for my mom,

Peggy Gilligan Van Sicklen,
whose love of fashion and design
have set me on this path.

Published in 2011 by Stewart, Tabori & Chang
An imprint of ABRAMS

Text and illustrations copyright © 2011 by Margaret Van Sicklen
Photographs copyright © 2011 by Jen Gotch

Library of Congress Cataloging-in-Publication Data

Van Sicklen, Margaret.
Modern paper crafts : a 21st-century guide to folding, cutting,
scoring, pleating, and recycling / Margaret Van Sicklen ;
photographs by Jen Gotch.
       p. cm.
Includes bibliographical references and index.
ISBN 978-1-58479-866-8 (alk. paper)
1. Paper work. I. Title.
   TT870.V365 2011
   736'.98--dc22
    2010016744

Editor: Melanie Falick
Technical Editor: Christine Timmons
Designer: onethread design, inc.
Production Manager: Tina Cameron

The text of this book was composed in Whitney and
ITC Lubalin Graph.

Printed and bound in China

10 9 8 7 6 5 4 3 2 1

Stewart, Tabori & Chang books are available at special discounts
when purchased in quantity for premiums and promotions as
well as fundraising or educational use. Special editions can also
be created to specification. For details, contact specialsales@
abramsbooks.com or the address below.

115 West 18th Street
New York, NY 10011
www.abramsbooks.com

MODERN
PAPER
CRAFTS

A 21st-Century Guide to Folding, Cutting, Scoring, Pleating, and Recycling

Margaret Van Sicklen

PHOTOGRAPHY BY JEN GOTCH

STC Craft | A Melanie Falick Book / Stewart, Tabori & Chang / New York

CONTENTS

INTRODUCTION

As far back as I can remember I have always enjoyed working with paper. As a kid, I was the one in the family who wrapped all the gifts. Actually, my real expertise was in unwrapping and then rewrapping. Always curious, I could untie the silkiest of bows, unwrap a package, and then wrap it up again, aligning all the creases without a trace. As a student, I loved painting, drawing, printmaking, and ceramics. I majored in fine art at Mills College in Oakland, California, and then went on to get a second degree in graphic arts at Parsons School of Design in New York.

After college, I worked as an art director in advertising of fashion and beauty products. At home I always had a stash of beautiful paper at the ready to make cards and party invitations. Because I am fascinated by how things work, I explored methods for creating cards with moving parts and dimensional features.

In 1998 I came up with the idea of combining origami with a page-a-day calendar format. Yesterday's page became the folding paper for the origami instructions on today's page—a simple recycling idea. It was a big success, which I think surprised everyone, especially me. I hadn't realized how many other paper folders were out there.

In *Modern Paper Crafts*, it has been a delight to use my favorite techniques—folding, cutting, scoring, and pleating—to make projects for the home and for giving. The last section of the book is about recycling, which is not really a technique, but is a great way to be both creative and eco-conscious.

Although the techniques featured in this book go far back in history, I strived to use them to create projects that feel fresh and modern. None of the projects are hard to make, even the ones with many steps, so please try out every one that intrigues you.

I hope that you will enjoy making the projects here and that they will inspire you to delve even further into paper crafting. Paper is an amazing medium that continually stirs my imagination. I hope it does the same for you.

Chapter 1

GETTING STARTED

understanding paper

The key material in paper crafting is, of course, paper, which is available in a stunning array of colors, patterns, sizes, and textures. In order to choose paper for your projects, it's helpful to understand some basic terminology.

Handmade Paper

Until the nineteenth century all paper was made by hand, one sheet at a time, in a process that is still practiced today: The craftsperson stands over a vat of macerated fibers (such as cotton, linen, or wood pulp) suspended in a watery solution. Using a wooden frame fitted with a fine-mesh screen, he or she scoops up the pulp and gives it a quick shake as the water quickly drains off, leaving a sheet of interconnected fibers. Next the wet sheet gets flipped out of the frame onto a felt mat and is then either air- or machine-dried.

Mould-Made Paper

Mould-made paper is machine-made paper that is made to look like handmade paper. There are a few clues to identify a mould-made sheet: The surface is more uniform than when handmade, the fibers align in one direction, there is a maximum of two deckled (feathered) edges, and it is less expensive than handmade paper.

Machine-Made Paper

Machine-made papers are mainly manufactured for commercial use and are consistent in size, quality, and color. There are many beautiful machine-made papers produced for specific end uses like printmaking, drawing, watercolor, origami, and publishing.

Bulk

Bulk refers to how thick or thin a paper is. To evaluate a paper's bulk, all you need to do is touch it. Card stock, artist papers, watercolor paper, scrapbook paper, Bristol board, and poster board are all popular bulky, or thick, papers. Standard origami paper, decorative papers (including many handmade papers), vellum, freezer paper, copy paper, and tissue paper are all thin papers.

Flexibility/Brittleness

Flexible paper is soft and floppy and can be worked and reworked with ease. Brittle paper is very stiff and is more challenging to rework. Flexibility and brittleness can be assessed by rattle, that is, the sound you hear when you hold a piece of paper by the corner and give it a shake. A brittle paper will make a sharp sound; a flexible paper will just wave in the air and make a swishing sound.

Grain

Both handmade and machine-made paper have grain, however the grain of handmade paper is random (meaning the fibers run in lots of different directions), while the grain of most machine-made paper is straight (since during the manufacturing process most of the fibers are aligned in the same direction). On machine-made paper, grain can run vertically or horizontally. Folding machine-made paper parallel to the grain will result in a clean, crisp crease; folding against the grain is possible, but more care must be taken to avoid rough creases and inaccurate folds. Because handmade papers have randomly placed fibers, they fold and tear with the same resistance in all directions.

If you've ever torn an article from the newspaper, you may have noticed that the paper tears nice and straight in one direction and ragged in the other direction. The straight tear is a result of tearing with the grain. To identify the direction of the grain, gently roll opposite long edges of the paper toward each other, then gently roll opposite short edges toward each other. You will notice that the paper is easier to roll in the direction of the grain. For projects that require only one or two folds, such as a greeting card, plan to make the folds along the grain. If a project has multiple folds in various directions, it is not necessary to plan folding with the grain.

ROW 1: GIFT WRAP, CORRUGATED CARDBOARD, GLASSINE, CHIYOGAMI (SILKSCREENED PATTERNED PAPER FROM JAPAN)

ROW 2: VELLUM, SCRAPBOOK PAPER, REPTILE-EMBOSSED PAPER, UNRYU (LIGHTWEIGHT TRANSLUCENT PAPER WITH LONG KOZO [MULBERRY] FIBERS)

ROW 3: ARTIST PAPER, CARD STOCK, NEWSPAPER, WATERCOLOR PAPER

ROW 4: KOZO (PAPER MADE FROM MULBERRY FIBERS), KRAFT PAPER, TRACING PAPER, ORIGAMI PAPER

Sizing

Sizing is a substance added to paper to help slow its absorption of moisture, so ink applied to the paper doesn't bleed. Sized paper is often stiffer and more brittle than unsized paper and holds a crease well. Unsized paper can be floppy (depending on its bulk); although it can be creased, it doesn't hold a crease well.

Acidity

Acid-free paper is paper that has been treated to be pH neutral. This treatment slows the process of degradation and reduces yellowing and brittleness (to which papers made from acidic fibers like wood pulp are subject). Generally, papers that are acid-free are labeled as such.

Finish

There is a variety of treatments that can be applied to papers, depending on the intended use and the desired characteristics. After the paper is made, it can be run through cylinders to produce various surface textures. Cold-press paper has a slightly rough surface; hot-press paper has a slick, smooth surface. Papers can be embossed with a texture, such as linen, which mimics the appearance of linen fabric. Papers can also be coated to give them matte or glossy finishes. Note that the texture of the paper can vary from one side to the other. Keep this in mind when working on projects where both sides of the paper may be visible.

choosing paper

Every project in this book can be successfully and beautifully made from common everyday papers, such as those you'd find at any office supply store. A wide assortment of suitable papers can also be found at art, craft, and scrapbook supply stores, as well as card and stationery shops. If you are exploring paper crafts for the first time, I suggest purchasing inexpensive poster board, copy paper, origami paper, scrapbook paper, and a roll of freezer paper to test the techniques—you'll also find specific recommendations for practice paper in each project.

The first time you create a project, use the type of paper recommended in the project's general Supplies list, as it is one that will perform well. Once you feel comfortable creating the project, feel free to experiment with specialty papers, such as handmade or mould-made paper, which may be more challenging to work with (see Understanding Paper on page 10 for information on the general categories and characteristics of paper). These papers often have subtler colors and richer textures, but some are more flexible, requiring them to be bonded to a backing paper for additional support (see Making Duo Paper on page 14). You may also find that the color of some of these papers changes when wet glue is applied or that the color bleeds when the paper gets wet. As you become more experienced working with specialty papers, you will find ways to make all their individual characteristics work in your favor.

If you are attracted to a paper with a printed pattern or in a special color, I suggest purchasing it right away when you see it. Specialty papers tend to follow design trends and are usually made in limited quantities.

Once you've worked with a paper, if possible, keep a swatch of it in a notebook with notes on its origin, fiber content, characteristics, where you bought it, and the project you made with it. The more you work with different papers, the easier it will be for you to predict how a new paper will perform, especially if you keep good notes.

storing paper

It is best to store your papers flat in a clean, dry place out of sunlight, because some papers are light-sensitive and may fade. If you have large handmade papers you can store them between the layers of a large flattened corrugated box under a bed. I like to organize my papers by type and use a sheet of poster board between the paper layers to separate the types. I like to store smaller papers together by size and type in lidded storage boxes or on paper storage shelves. Some special storage shelves are available for storing 12"-square scrapbook papers.

Although it is preferable to store papers flat, you can roll large sheets and store them in mailing tubes; just be sure the paper clings to the inside of the tube, rather than being rolled up tight resting on its end, to prevent damaging the edges of the paper. Another option is to roll paper around the outside of a tube that is longer than the paper is wide (so that the edges of the paper don't get damaged). Before using the rolled papers, allow them to relax or smooth them out and weight them down with books until they are flat again.

STEP 1: PLACE FIRST SHEET OF PAPER, FACE DOWN, ON WORK SURFACE, AND SPRAY ADHESIVE ON IT. THEN ALIGN SECOND SHEET OF PAPER, FACE UP, ON FIRST SHEET.

STEP 2: PRESS LAYERS TOGETHER WITH BRUSH OR YOUR HANDS TO SMOOTH OUT ANY AIR BUBBLES IN ADHESIVE.

making duo paper

Duo paper consists of two sheets of paper that are adhered to each other to make one sheet. You would choose to make duo paper for one of two reasons: First, a project requires a bulky paper, but you fell in love with a sheet of thin paper that is too flimsy for the project you want to make. In this case, you can adhere two layers of the same paper together to make it suitably bulky for your project. (This is what I did for the Op Art Mobile on page 78 and the Flower Pot/Vase Cover on page 70). Or you can adhere a lightweight paper to a more durable one for added strength and body (as I did for the Garland Chain on page 66). The second reason you may want to make duo paper is to create a custom paper. In this case, you might choose two papers with different qualities—varying colors, textures, or patterns—and adhere them together. There are two different methods for creating duo paper, using spray adhesive or methyl cellulose.

DUO PAPER: SPRAY-ADHESIVE METHOD

Use the spray-adhesive method of creating duo paper when you want to combine two sheets of paper without getting them wet. The advantage of this method is that both the process and drying time are fast. I find this method of making duo paper works best with machine-made paper. Set up your spray station in a well-ventilated area. I prefer doing this outside, if possible.

After the papers are adhered together and the adhesive is dry, you will be able to feel the thin layer of glue between the sheets which changes the original characteristics of the paper. This is sometimes a good thing and sometimes not.

Materials and Tools
2 sheets of paper
Newsprint
Spray adhesive
Approximately 6"-wide brush (optional)

Instructions
1. Cover a large work area with newsprint, because the mist travels. Place a sheet of paper, face down, on the newsprint. Apply the spray adhesive to the back side of the paper, following the manufacturer's instructions printed on the can.

2. Lay a second sheet of paper, face up, on the first sheet, aligning the edges, and press the layers together with the brush or your hands, smoothing out any air bubbles. Let the duo paper dry.

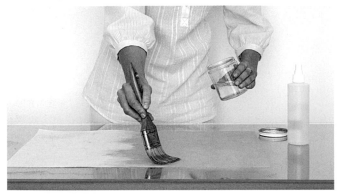

STEPS 1-3: SPRITZ FIRST SHEET OF PAPER WITH WATER ON BOTH SIDES, AND LAY ON WORK SURFACE. THEN MIX AND BRUSH ON METHYL CELLULOSE GLUE.

DUO PAPER: METHYL CELLULOSE METHOD

Methyl cellulose is a water-soluble, clear-drying bookbinding adhesive that is acid-free. It works well on handmade papers; however, it should be tested on a scrap of paper first to check for color bleeding or change in texture. If the paper changes in an undesirable way, use the spray-adhesive method for creating duo paper. The advantage of this method over the spray-adhesive method is that the bonded papers feel as though they have become one, and you don't feel the layer of glue between the layers of paper.

Materials and Tools

Methyl cellulose powder (see Resources on page 142)
Water
Jar or bowl
Wooden stir stick
Drop cloth
Glass or Plexiglas work surface, such as a frame
    with a glass or Plexiglas insert
Spray bottle with water
2 sheets of paper
Approximately 6"-wide brush, for smoothing paper
Approximately 2"-wide, clean paintbrush, for applying adhesive
X-Acto knife
Stack of books (optional)

Instructions

1. Gradually mix the methyl cellulose powder with cool, clean water in a jar or bowl, following the ratio listed on the product label. Stir continuously until all the powder is dissolved. The water will get cloudy, and some clumps may form in the bottom. Let the solution rest overnight. The trapped bubbles will disappear, and the liquid will become crystal clear and glossy. It should be as thick as shampoo or liquid hand soap. If it is too thick, you can thin it down by gradually adding a little more cool water and gently stirring it together. Or, if it is too thin, add more methyl cellulose powder, and let it rest again before use.

2. Cover a large work area with a drop cloth, and place the glass or Plexiglas surface on the drop cloth. Lightly spritz one sheet of paper on both sides with water. Lay the paper down on the glass or Plexiglas surface. With a wide brush, smooth the paper so it is nice and flat and void of air bubbles and creases.

STEP 4: SPRITZ AND ALIGN SECOND SHEET OVER FIRST, BRUSHING ENTIRE SURFACE TO SMOOTH IT AND PUSH OUT AIR BUBBLES.

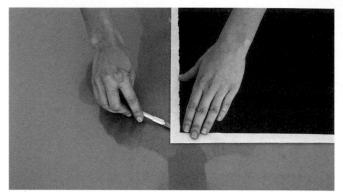

STEP 5: IF NECESSARY, USE X-ACTO KNIFE TO RELEASE CORNER OF DRIED DUO PAPER FROM WORK SURFACE.

3. Dip the paintbrush into the methyl cellulose, and brush the adhesive onto the paper, starting in one corner and moving across the paper. Imagine that you are applying a sticker and want to get out all the air bubbles. You'll get better at this with just a little practice. Brush a layer of methyl cellulose evenly across the entire surface of the paper. Brush the methyl cellulose over the edges of the paper too, so the sheet is adhered to the glass or Plexiglas surface.

4. Lightly spritz the second sheet of paper on both sides with the spray bottle. Lay the second sheet of paper on top of the first one, aligning the edges, and, with a wide brush, go over the entire surface of the sheet, smoothing it down and pushing the air bubbles out through the sides. Let the paper air-dry overnight.

5. Carefully peel the paper off the glass or Plexiglas surface. If the paper seems to be stuck, use an X-Acto knife to release one corner, and slowly pull the paper up away from the surface. You will notice the side of the paper adhered to the glass is smoother and slightly shiny compared to the other side, which is matte and textured. If the paper curls, weight it down overnight with a stack of books, and it will flatten out.

tools and materials

The following list describes the items that I use when creating projects from paper. You may not need all the items in this list, depending on the projects you choose to make.

MEASURING TOOLS

Straightedge Ruler

An 18" or 24" steel ruler is my ruler of choice. It is a good length for measuring and makes an excellent straight edge when used along with an X-Acto knife to produce precise cuts. Aluminum and plastic rulers are less expensive, but they become nicked and chipped over time, which will lead to rough cuts and inaccurate measurements.

Triangle Ruler

Triangle rulers have three straight edges. I use a clear acrylic, gridded, right-angle triangular ruler with a steel edge. This type of ruler works well for trimming large pieces of paper into smaller squares and rectangles. The right angle of the ruler can be placed at the corner of the paper to check for proper alignment. If the edges of the cut paper align with the edges of the ruler, you will know that the paper was cut at a 90-degree angle. If the edges don't align, it will be necessary to make a straightening cut on the edge of the paper that doesn't align with the ruler. The steel edge is an important feature and helps to ensure accurate marking and cutting. Clear gridded triangle rulers are tools sometimes used by quilters. Please note, however, that these rulers don't have a steel edge and aren't always right-angle rulers.

T-Square

A T-square is a measuring tool shaped like the letter T. I prefer an 18" or 24" stainless-steel T-square, which works well for marking and trimming large sheets of paper. To do this, first tape your paper to your work surface, next align the short edge of the T-square along the edge of your work surface, then mark or cut along an edge of the long arm of the tool. The stainless-steel edge ensures that your marking and cutting will be precise.

Avoid T-squares made from other materials, as the straight edges can become marred over time, leading to less than perfect results.

CUTTING TOOLS

Scissors

Utility Scissors

An 8"-long utility scissors with a safe, blunt tip is a must-have, general-purpose scissors. I use this tool for trimming large sheets of paper to more usable sizes.

Small, Pointed-Tip Scissors

You can use any short, pointed-tip scissors, but my favorites are Fiskars Micro-Tip scissors. Their overall length is 5", and their blades measure 1¾" long. The blades are very pointed at the tip and sharp right to the very end, making them great for snipping into small places.

Manicure Scissors

A manicure scissors is a small scissors with short curved blades. It is my favorite tool for cutting small silhouettes, because it can be moved into tight places, and the curved blade makes it easy to trim around shapes with small curves.

Decorative Paper Scissors

Decorative paper scissors, available in craft and scrapbooking stores, have blades capable of producing a specific decorative cut edge, including scalloped, faux deckled, pinked, or wavy. I used a pinking scissors to produce a zigzag edge on the Wine-Bottle Daisy Frill (see page 54).

Other Cutting Tools

Rotary Cutter

A rotary cutter is a handheld device with a round, sharp blade, similar to a pizza cutter. It makes straight cuts quickly and effortlessly. It is used in combination with a cutting mat, which is placed under the paper during the cutting process to protect the work surface. Replace the blade when it becomes dull.

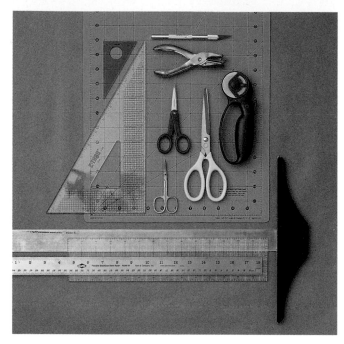

MEASURING AND CUTTING TOOLS

When working on projects made out of corrugated cardboard, the blade will dull quickly. You may want to add a rubber pencil grip to the metal stick that holds the blade, as it will make the knife more comfortable to hold. It also helps to prevent the knife from rolling off your work surface.

Cutting Mat

A cutting mat is an essential tool for paper crafts. It will save your tabletop from cuts, and many provide a flexible, nonslip surface that holds the paper secure when working. Be sure to use a self-healing cutting mat. This type of mat shows no marring on the surface after repeated uses. If you use a mat that is not self-healing, over time you will end up with cut lines and a rough texture on the surface of the mat, which can mar your paper and cause inaccurate cuts. If you use a mat with a printed measurement grid, you will save a lot of time when measuring and trimming paper.

The smallest cutting mat I recommend is 12" wide x 16" long. The advantage of a small cutting mat is that you can tape your paper to it and then rotate the mat into different positions to make cutting with an X-Acto knife more comfortable. After many years I broke down and purchased a large cutting mat. It measures 24" wide x 36" long and is a luxury I enjoy. A large cutting mat makes it easy to cut large, beautiful art papers down to a usable size; it can also save you time when measuring and cutting since it allows you to work in one continuous motion instead of having to shift the paper as you run out of space on a smaller mat.

Hole Punch

Handheld hole punches with spring action are used to cut small images from paper. The variety of styles and images available has expanded with the popularity of scrapbooking, but for the projects in this book, you'll only need a ⅛"-round punch.

X-Acto Knife

An X-Acto knife consists of a metal stick holder, similar in shape and size to a pencil, with a removable blade at the end. Always use an X-Acto knife with a cutting mat to prevent damaging your work surface, and run it along the steel edge of a ruler to create precise cuts in paper. When the blade becomes dull, replace it with a new one. Purchase standard (size 11) blades in containers of 100, which are economical and will mean that you won't hesitate to change the blade when it gets dull. Your projects will look better when cut with a fresh blade, and accidents will be prevented by not working with a dull tool.

Scoring Tools

A scoring tool is drawn across the surface of the paper while applying pressure to create an indent, or score line. Scoring breaks down the fibers for the purpose of pre-creasing the paper at a location where a fold is to be made. This step helps ensure a neat and accurate fold. Any thin-bladed, dull metal object, such as a fish or butter knife, can be used for scoring. It's important to use a dull tool to avoid cutting the paper when creating score lines.

When scoring paper, it is helpful to work on a surface that has a bit of give, so as you're scoring the paper, it can sink into the surface. A cork board makes a great scoring mat and so does a thick pad of newsprint.

Burnishing Tools

A burnishing tool is used for rubbing over an existing paper fold that needs an extra-sharp crease. Smooth steady pressure makes the crease clean and sharp. The most popular burnisher is a "bone" folder, which is a 1"-wide, fairly flat tool often made out of plastic and measuring about 6" long, with a pointed tip on one end. Personally, however, I prefer wooden clay modeling tools for burnishing, as I tend to hold things tightly, and I find wood to be most comfortable in my hand. Look for reasonably priced, wooden tools that can serve as burnishing tools in the clay section of an art supply store.

Wet Adhesives

White Tacky Glue

White tacky glue is an all-purpose glue, similar to white liquid glue, such as Elmer's brand, but thicker and tackier. It dries quickly and, because it is thick, prevents papers from slipping out of position, and minimizes drips. I like Aleene's Tacky Glue.

Methyl Cellulose

This type of adhesive is used for making duo paper (see page 15). It dries clear and is water-soluble and acid-free.

Dry Adhesives

Masking Tape/Drafting Tape

This tape is wonderful for temporarily securing paper to your cutting mat. It tears off the roll by hand, pulls up easily from your cutting mat, and is reusable a couple of times.

Removable Tape

Removable tape is a low-tack, repositionable, clear tape that works well on delicate papers, as it will not damage the finish of the paper. I use Scotch brand removable tape, which is easily identifiable, because it comes on a blue spool. It is clear, making it easy to see through when positioning it.

Glue Stick

Glue sticks are good for small areas, such as on the Wine-Bottle Daisy Frill (page 54), or for when you only need one stroke of glue. Be careful that you replace the cap immediately after use. If the cap is left off for any length of time, the glue becomes a stretchy, lumpy mess when applied. Test the condition of your glue stick on a scrap of paper before using.

Adhesive Dots

Adhesive dots are little dots of gummy adhesive that come on a roll. They are available in a variety of sizes and can be flat or dimensional. There are also permanent and repositionable

varieties. For best results, follow the manufacturer's recommendations for using them. They can be tricky to apply but are very strong and handy for tight places, such as on the Flower Pot/Vase Cover (page 70).

Spray Adhesive

Spray adhesive works well for adhering two papers together when making duo paper (see page 14). It is sprayed onto the paper surface in a fine mist.

Craft Putty

Aleene's Acid-Free Craft Tack reusable craft putty is a wonderful, non-staining, archival putty that can be used as a permanent adhesive. It is perfect for some of the scored paper projects in this book, such as the Baroque Mirror Frame (page 102), as it can be shaped to help support the shaped paper. It can be repositioned as often as necessary until you find the perfect placement—and you can leave it in place since it hardens with time.

Pencil

Because mechanical pencils are always sharp, they are accurate for marking paper. I sometimes use a mechanical pencil, but I prefer a regular wood pencil, because I hold the pencil so tightly I tend to break the lead on mechanical pencils often.

Pencil Sharpener

Keep handy for shaping the pencil lead to a sharp point.

Eraser

Use an eraser to remove any unwanted marking lines. I like the Magic Rub brand of eraser because it is nonabrasive and removes all traces of lead without marring the paper's surface.

Binder Clips

Binder clips are strong clips with a thin, wide mouth that work well for temporarily holding materials firmly in position.

Assorted Brushes

I use a 2"-wide paintbrush and a 6"-wide drafting brush when making duo paper (see page 14).

Tiny Wooden Clothespins with Springs

These small clothespins work well for holding small, fragile items in place. They measure 1¾" long x ¼" wide. They work well on the Spring Branches (page 40) because the soft grip doesn't scar the paper.

Paper Towels

Paper towels come in handy for wiping up glue, especially when working with methyl cellulose. After cleaning paintbrushes, I wrap the wet bristles in a paper towel to keep them aligned while they dry.

Empty Beverage Can

The safest way to dispose of used X-Acto knife blades is in a clean, empty beverage can. A blade too dull for paper can still be hazardous to your flesh, so don't just toss the old blades into the trash. Pick a good-looking can, as it will take years to fill.

First-Aid Supplies

An antibiotic cream and adhesive bandages are good to have handy when working with cutting tools. If you apply too much pressure when you are cutting with an X-Acto knife, it is possible for the ruler to slip and you could cut yourself. Always be careful.

workspace

The best workspace has a flat work surface with good overhead lighting. A kitchen table or desk is often a good spot. Be sure the work surface is slightly larger than your paper and cutting mat, with ample room for supplies, such as rulers, cutting tools, and adhesives. The work surface should be clean and dry, as a grease spot or a bump from folding atop a cookie crumb is never welcome.

Overhead lighting that does not cast a strong shadow on the workspace is best for precise measurements, accurate folding, and safe cutting.

Always be sure that your hands are clean and free of oils. If your hands become dirty from pencil smudges or glue, take time out to wash and dry them thoroughly to prevent damaging the papers with which you are working.

Chapter 2

FOLDING

Folding involves the simplest of actions but can change a flat piece of paper into a three-dimensional one, producing something as basic as a box or as complex as a multi-petal flower. The art of folding paper is often referred to as origami, a Japanese word that means paper folding (*ori* meaning "to fold" and *kami* meaning "paper").

Today origami is enjoyed by hobbyists and artists around the world. It is also used in classrooms to teach children dexterity, mathematical concepts, and how to follow instructions. Origami purists frown on the use of scissors or glue and instead create all of their models through folding alone, typically starting with a square piece of paper.

Famous paper folders include magician Harry Houdini, author Lewis Carroll, and, one of the most famous, Curious George. In the popular children's book *Curious George Rides a Bike* by H. A. Rey, a monkey named George makes boats from newspapers and sails them down the river.

SETTING UP A WORKSPACE FOR FOLDING

To get started folding you'll need a smooth, flat, well-lit surface, at least slightly larger than the paper you plan to fold and with enough elbow room to move around comfortably. A cleared-off desk or kitchen table is often a good place. Be sure the surface is clean and dry, as paper is very sensitive to moisture. Also be sure your hands are clean and dry. Good overhead lighting that does not cast a strong shadow is important, as many times you will fold to previously made crease lines, which can be difficult to see without proper lighting. Folding the paper at exactly the right spot will produce accurate results.

BEST PAPERS FOR FOLDING

Projects that require multiple folds are best made with thin papers that hold a crease well. Classic origami requires multiple folds; therefore, origami paper is typically a strong, thin paper that holds a sharp crease. Other papers that hold a crease well include copy paper, scrapbook paper, and freezer paper. Scrapbook papers are fun to work with because they are available in lots of patterns and colors, are inexpensive compared to specialty papers, and can be purchased in single sheets.

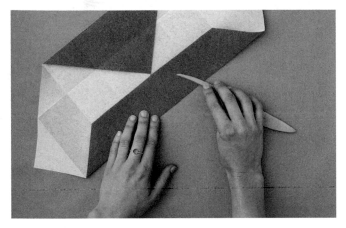

FOLDING WITH BURNISHING TOOL

Avoid papers that have a hard coating, such as some wrapping papers, because when folded repeatedly, these papers often produce surface cracks, leaving a white line. You can test any paper by folding back a corner and checking to see how the paper reacts. Use caution with wallpapers, vellum, and construction papers because they are brittle and may crack—test them and learn their individual limitations.

Thick paper is generally not recommended because it becomes bulky when folded, making it difficult for the paper layers to remain flat and making it impossible to achieve crisp, sharp creases. When thick papers are folded, the edges of the paper tend to creep out of alignment, which results in inaccurate folding. It is possible to achieve folding success with a thick paper if the project only has a few folds. However, the more folds needed to complete a project, the thinner the paper should be.

Patterned paper can be challenging to use on folded projects. The pattern can make it difficult to see the crease lines, which are sometimes used as landmarks for future folds. If you find it difficult to see crease lines, try holding the paper at an angle under your light source.

TOOLS FOR FOLDING PAPER

The best folding tools are your fingertips with their sense of touch and ability to manipulate. If you have strong nails, you also have a built-in burnisher. Simply draw your fingernail along the length of the fold line to create a crisp, sharp crease. Be aware that nail polish leaves scuff marks that are impossible to erase. If using your nail as a burnisher, stick to clear polish or none at all.

A plastic "bone" folder is one of the most common burnishing tools for achieving a crisp, sharp crease, especially when folding stiff paper, such as card stock. After the paper is folded, run the narrow side edge of the bone folder across the fold with even pressure to create a sharp crease line. Be careful not to over-burnish, especially with brittle paper, such as vellum, as it will cause the paper to crack and split open along the fold.

Wooden tools intended for use with clay can be very good burnishing tools. I find that wood is more comfortable in my hand than plastic, and because wooden tools are completely smooth there is little risk of creating scratch marks on the paper.

For more information on all of these tools, see page 19.

FOLDING SYMBOLS

The system of picture symbols used to illustrate origami instructions today is called the Yoshizawa-Randlett system. Developed in the 1950s, it is based on the work of Akira Yoshizawa, a Japanese origami master who developed a code of lines and arrows. Samuel Randlett, an American paper folder, and Robert Harbin, the first president of the British Origami Society, adopted the symbols of Akira Yoshizawa with some minor changes, resulting in a comprehensive set of symbols that has become the standard for origami. The Yoshizawa-Randlett system allows paper folders around the world to share instructions, regardless of the language they speak. On pages 26 and 27 you'll find the symbols used in this book, starting with the most common ones.

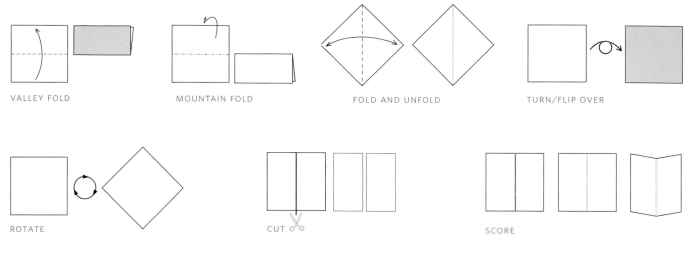

VALLEY FOLD MOUNTAIN FOLD FOLD AND UNFOLD TURN/FLIP OVER

ROTATE CUT SCORE

Valley Fold

A dashed line means to make a valley fold, which, when completed, resembles a valley.

Mountain Fold

A dash-dot-dash line means to make a mountain fold, which, when completed, resembles a mountain.

Fold and Unfold

A line with an arrowhead at both ends means to fold and unfold the paper, either for a valley or mountain fold (as indicated by marked fold line). The result of folding and unfolding is a crease, or solid straight line. Folding and unfolding is often used to prepare for a future maneuver.

Turn/Flip Over

This symbol indicates that the paper should be turned or flipped over from one side to the other. When the paper is face up, it is shown as colored. When the paper is face down, it is shown as white.

Rotate

A circle with multiple arrowheads tells you to reorient the paper in the direction noted in text (either clockwise or counterclockwise) to prepare for the next step.

Cut

A red line with scissors indicates where to cut the paper (see Tips for Cutting Paper on page 52). If a drawing has multiple cut lines, the scissors will appear only with one of these lines.

Score

A blue line indicates a line to be scored (see Tips for Scoring Paper on page 87). Once scored, the paper is folded along the scored line, which is shown as two lightweight parallel lines.

Sink/Push In

A solid arrowhead above a point means to sink, or push in, the point neatly, using the existing crease lines.

Star

A star is a reference point, showing either where to fold a line or point, or where to firmly hold the paper when following the directions in a step.

Open Out

An outlined arrow means to open up or pull out the area or layer that the arrow points to.

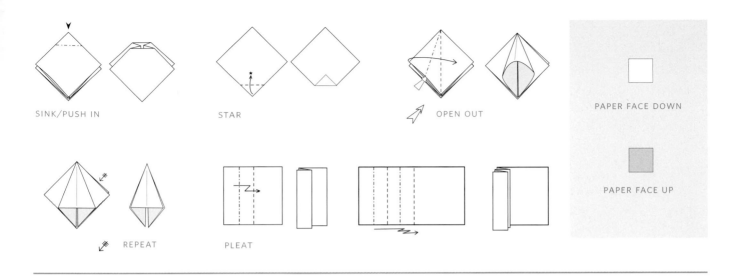

SINK/PUSH IN   STAR   OPEN OUT   PAPER FACE DOWN

REPEAT   PLEAT   PAPER FACE UP

Repeat

An arrow with one or more cross-stroke lines on its tail means to repeat the directions in a step where indicted, with the number of cross-strokes denoting the number of repetitions called for. Here, the repeat symbol means to open and flatten out the remaining three folded panels of this form.

Pleat

An arrow with a zigzag tail calls for making alternating mountain and valley folds to produce pleats.

TIPS FOR FOLDING PAPER

I find that it usually takes three tries to fold a perfect model. To begin, practice with the suggested practice paper in the project's Supplies list, which will be similar in weight to the actual paper recommended for the project. Or, if the actual paper you've chosen for your project is inexpensive and you have plenty of it, go ahead and use it for practice. Note, too, that if you selected a final paper that's patterned on one side and solid on the other, you should choose a similarly patterned/solid paper for practice. On the first try, familiarize yourself with the sequence of folding steps. On the second try, focus on accuracy. If you feel comfortable with the result of your second attempt, fold the project with the paper selected for the final project on the third try. You will see a big difference in accuracy and artistry between the first try and the third try. If you take your time, the process will be relaxing and the results will be more enjoyable than if you rush or expect too much of yourself at the outset.

It is especially important for the first fold of a project to be accurate. If the first fold is off, the remaining folds will all be off as well, and the degree of inaccuracy will increase with each step.

Before beginning a project, review the step-by-step diagrams for that project. After completing each step, look at the next diagram to see if what you've created matches what is shown.

In general, I recommend following the folding diagrams exactly as they appear with each project. If, however, you find it easier to rotate the model to a different position to make the fold, go ahead. Just be sure to reposition the model as shown in the diagram when you move on to the next step.

Candy Cones

In days gone by, candy was scooped from large glass jars at the market into paper cones like these. Today I like to use them to add a special touch at parties for both children and adults. To make larger cones that can be used instead of a gift box (for light items like handknitted mittens and socks), simply start with a bigger piece of paper in the same proportions (its width should be 2¼ times its height). For example, for a 6" tall cone, cut a rectangle 13½" wide x 6" tall.

FINISHED SIZE
About 4" wide at top x 5½" tall at point

SUPPLIES
Practice paper: 1 sheet of copy paper

1 sheet of lightweight paper, cut to 9" wide x 4" tall

Ruler

Pencil

PAPERS SHOWN

I made the patterned cones with wrapping paper, the solid-colored cones with art paper, and the striped cones with scrapbook paper.

Directions

1. Position the paper horizontally face down. Using a ruler and measuring 8" in from the left edge, lightly pencil-mark a reference line at this point (when you get to be a candy-cone pro, you won't need the reference mark).

2. Fold (see Tips for Folding Paper on page 27) the paper's left edge to the 8" reference line, and then unfold the paper. Next fold the paper's right edge at the 8" reference line, and then unfold it.

3. Fold the top left corner down to meet the bottom edge.

4. Fold the bottom left corner over to the 8" crease line.

5. Lightly roll the bottom left corner up to meet the top edge of the 8" crease line.

6. Gently squeeze the left side of the cone to open it, and fold the 1" flap inside this open edge to lock the cone into shape.

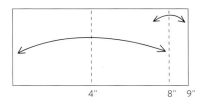

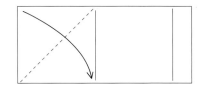

1 MEASURE AND MARK.

2 FOLD LEFT SIDE TO MARK; FOLD RIGHT SIDE AT MARK, AND UNFOLD.

3 FOLD CORNER.

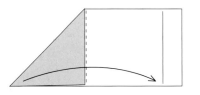

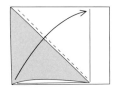

4 FOLD TO MARK.

5 ROLL OVER TO MARK.

6a SQUEEZE OPEN AND FOLD FLAP OVER.

6b FINISHED CONE.

Organizer Trays

Our lives are filled with lots of miscellanea and these simple trays make keeping track of it all a lot easier. Place one or two next to the door to hold keys, lipsticks, jewelry, and/or any other trinkets you might like to pick up or put down as you enter and exit the house. Try another on your dresser or next to the bed. And, of course, you'll need some for notes, clips, and pens and pencils on your desk. You can even use these trays to hold bread, napkins, silverware, or other buffet items at the dining room table.

FINISHED SIZE

Note: In dimensions throughout, width precedes length.

Small: 2½" x 6½" x 1¼"
Medium: 3½" x 8¼" x 1¾"
Large: 4⅛" x 9½" x 2"
Extra-large: 5½" x 12" x 2¾"

SUPPLIES

Practice paper: 12" square of scrapbook paper

1 sheet of 9" x 10" (small), 11½" x 13¼" (medium), 15" x 18" (large), 17" x 21" (extra-large) poster board or card stock

Bone or wood folder

X-Acto knife

PAPERS SHOWN

To make these boxes, I used reptile-embossed coated papers from Taiwan.

Notes: The larger the tray you want to make, the sturdier the paper should be. If you use paper that's patterned or colored on one side only, note that a face-down triangle of paper will show at the center of each short end of the completed tray.

Directions

1. Position the poster board or card stock horizontally face up, and fold (see Tips for Folding Paper on page 27) it in half lengthwise. Burnish the folded edge firmly with the bone folder; then unfold the card stock or board.

2. Fold both the right and left edges into the center crease. Burnish the folded edges firmly; then unfold the edges.

3. Cut off the far right panel.

4. Fold the right edge to the left crease.

5. Fold the right flap in half. Burnish the folded edge firmly; then unfold the flap.

6. Firmly fold all four corners on the right flap to the flap's center crease. Burnish the folded edges sharply.

7. Fold the left edge of the flap to the right along the existing center crease.

8. Fold the far left edge over to align with the far right edge, using the existing crease line.

9. Fold the top flap in half. Burnish the folded edge firmly; then unfold the flap.

1 FOLD IN HALF, AND UNFOLD.

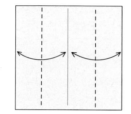

2 FOLD BOTH EDGES TO CENTER, AND UNFOLD.

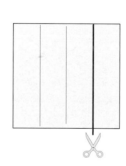

3 CUT OFF FAR RIGHT PANEL.

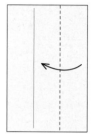

4 FOLD RIGHT EDGE TO LEFT CREASE.

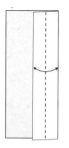

5 FOLD RIGHT FLAP IN HALF, AND UNFOLD.

6 FOLD ALL FOUR CORNERS TO CENTER CREASE.

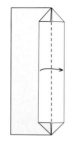

7 FOLD FLAP'S LEFT EDGE TO RIGHT EDGE.

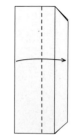

8 FOLD FAR LEFT EDGE TO RIGHT EDGE.

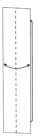

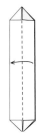

9 FOLD TOP FLAP IN HALF, AND UNFOLD.

10 FOLD ALL FOUR CORNERS TO CENTER CREASE.

11 FOLD TOP FLAP'S RIGHT EDGE TO LEFT EDGE.

12 FOLD TOP AND BOTTOM POINTS TO CENTER, AND UNFOLD.

13 OPEN UP BOX AT CENTER.

10. Firmly fold all four corners of top flap to that flap's center crease. Burnish the folded edges sharply.

11. Fold the right half of the top flap to align it with the left edge, using the existing crease line.

12. Fold down the top and bottom points toward the center, and burnish all the corner edges firmly. Unfold the points.

13. Open up the folded box at the center to pop it into shape. Give all the corners a little pinch to make them sharp.

Treat Boxes

Next time you're taking treats to a friend's house, pack them in one of these boxes to make your gift extra-special. The boxes shown may look small, but you can actually pack a good selection of fudge, brownies, or cookies inside of them (alternatively, you can make your boxes bigger by starting with a larger square of paper). I like to line my boxes with baking parchment paper, so any moisture from my treats won't discolor it.

FINISHED SIZE

6½" square x 3¼" tall

SUPPLIES

Practice paper: 18" square of medium-weight card stock

18" square of medium-weight card stock or specialty paper

Bone or wood folder

Notes: You can start with any size square of paper, and the resulting box will be about one-third the size of the starting square. The larger the box you want to make, the sturdier the paper should be.

PAPERS SHOWN

For the boxes shown, I used three Japanese papers: blue silk-screened chiyogami paper, brown silkscreened mulberry paper, and handmade yellow mulberry paper.

Directions

TREAT BOX BOTTOM

1. Position the paper face up, and fold (see Tips for Folding Paper on page 27) it in half, from side to side. Use your bone folder to crease the folds firmly (burnishing the folded edges sharply in this and the next step is important for shaping the box). Unfold the paper.

2. Fold the paper in half, from top to bottom, and crease the folds firmly. Unfold the paper. Flip the paper over, so it's face down.

3. Using the crease lines as guides, fold all the corners to the center. Hold the paper firmly in place while creasing the new fold lines since card stock tends to slip out of alignment.

4. Fold the top and bottom edges to meet in the center, rolling each edge back and forth a few times as you bring it to the center to help the thick paper fold smoothly. Burnish each of the folded edges firmly. Unfold the paper.

TREAT BOX BOTTOM

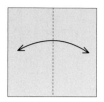

1 FOLD IN HALF, AND UNFOLD.

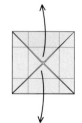

2 FOLD IN HALF, AND UNFOLD.
FLIP OVER.

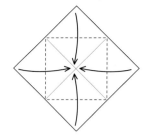

3 FOLD CORNERS TO CENTER.

4 FOLD TO CENTER,
AND UNFOLD.

5 FOLD TO CENTER,
AND UNFOLD.

6 OPEN OUT.

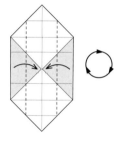

7 FOLD TO CENTER,
AND ROTATE.

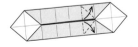

8 OPEN SIDE FLAPS TO
STAND UP.

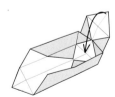

9 FOLD POINT OVER EDGE.

10 REPEAT STEPS 8-9 ON OPEN END.

4L FOLLOW STEPS 1-3 FOR BOX BOTTOM; THEN FOLD TO JUST SHY OF CENTER, AND UNFOLD.

5L FOLD TO JUST SHY OF CENTER, AND UNFOLD.

6L OPEN OUT. CONTINUE WITH STEPS 7-10 FOR BOX BOTTOM.

---

5. Fold the right and left edges to meet in the center. As before, roll each edge a couple times as you bring it to the center, and burnish the folded edges firmly. Unfold the paper.

6. Unfold the top and bottom sections.

7. Fold the outer right and left edges to the center on the existing crease lines. Rotate the folded shape, so it's horizontal.

8. Open the side flaps so that they stand up (here's when the box starts to pop up into shape). Gently push the sides together. The end point will lift up.

9. Fold the end point over the edge, so it meets the center of the box.

10. To finish shaping the box, repeat steps 8-9 on the remaining open end.

TREAT BOX LID

1-3. To make a lid for the treat box that's slightly larger than the box bottom so that it's easy to remove (very helpful if you're working with thick paper), first follow steps 1-3 for the treat box bottom above.

4. Then, following Step 4L, fold the top and bottom edges toward the center but just shy of it, stopping at the star about ⅜" away from it. (Note that this distance is variable and up to you, but be sure to fold all four sides the same distance. Note, too, that this distance determines how much you'll enlarge the box lid and shorten its sides.) While folding each edge, roll it back and forth a few times to help the thick paper fold smoothly. Burnish each of the folded edges firmly, and unfold the paper.

5. Following Step 5L, fold the right and left edges toward the center but just shy of it, again stopping at the star. Again roll each edge a couple times as you bring it to the center. Burnish the folded edges firmly, and unfold the paper.

6. Following Step 6L, unfold the top and bottom sections.

7-10. Continue with steps 7-10 for constructing the treat box bottom to complete the lid.

Note: After you get the hang of making this box and lid, you may want to avoid the X crease mark that appears on the top of the lid. To do this, skip the folding steps 1-2 when making the lid, and start with Step 3, folding carefully in the absence of crease marks.

Spring Branches

Everyone's face brightens when the dogwood trees bloom in early spring. Create that happy springtime feeling in your home any time of year with these budding paper flowers. I used coffee filters to make these flowers because I knew their wonderful, crepe-like texture would give them a soft, natural look. If you like, you can use a little watercolor paint to vary each one (see page 47).

FINISHED SIZE
Flower: 3" diameter
Leaf: 2" long x 1½" wide

SUPPLIES
Practice paper: 1 sheet of origami or other thin paper

Ten #4 white cone coffee filters

Scraps of card stock for templates, cut to 3½" x 1¾" for flower (F) and 2" square for leaf (L)

Utility scissors

Bone or wood folder

Pencil

Hot glue gun

Tree branch

Watercolors (see page 47)

Directions

FOR LEAVES AND FLOWER
Note: One coffee filter makes two leaves and one flower.

1. To cut two leaf patterns from a coffee filter, first position and trace the flower template (F) as follows: Place F on the filter's folded edge, and trace around it with a pencil. Next place the leaf template (L) alongside the traced flower template, as shown in Drawing 1, and trace around L. Cut out the tracings, which will yield one square (when opened) for a flower and two squares for leaves. Set the flower square and one of the leaf squares aside for now.

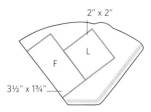

2" x 2"

L

F

3½" x 1¾"

1 TRACE TEMPLATES AND CUT.

2 FOLD IN HALF.

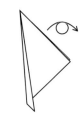

3a FOLD EDGE OVER
AT SHARP ANGLE.

3b FLIP OVER.

4 FOLD AND UNFOLD.

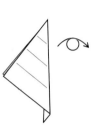

5a FOLD AND UNFOLD.

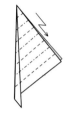

5b FLIP OVER.

6a ACCORDIAN-PLEAT LEAF,
FOLDING EACH SECTION
IN HALF TO CREASED
LINE BELOW.

6b UNFOLD LEAF.

7 FOLD TOP LAYER'S
BOTTOM RIGHT CORNER;
REPEAT ON OTHER SIDE.

FOR LEAVES

2. Position the leaf square on point, and fold (see Tips for Folding Paper on page 27) it in half.

3. Fold the left folded edge over to the right on a slight angle. Flip the leaf over.

4. Fold the triangle's top point down to meet its left point, and unfold it.

5. Fold the top point down to meet the center crease you just made, and unfold it. Then fold the left point up to meet the center crease, and unfold it. Flip the leaf over.

6. Accordion-pleat the leaf forward and backward by first folding the top point down to the first creased line and then folding each section below in half to the next creased line below. Unfold the leaf.

7. Fold over the top layer only of the bottom right point. Then repeat this step on the other side.

8 REFOLD ACCORDIAN
  PLEATS.

9 CREASE FOLDS
  FIRMLY.

10a OPEN.

10b SHAPE LEAF.

8. With the bottom points still folded back, refold the accordion pleats.

9. Crease the folds firmly with a bone folder.

10. Open the leaf slowly, so it retains its creases like a fresh new leaf in spring.

Repeat steps 2-10 to make the second leaf from the square you cut and set aside.

FLOWER

1 TRACE AND CUT.

2 OPEN.

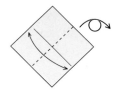

3 FOLD IN HALF, AND UNFOLD.
FLIP OVER.

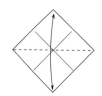

4 FOLD IN HALF,
AND UNFOLD.

5 FOLD IN HALF, AND UNFOLD.
FLIP OVER.

6a COLLAPSE ON
EXISTING CREASES.

6b COLLAPSED SQUARE.

7 CREASE FOLDS FIRMLY.

8 FOLD AND UNFOLD
TOP LAYER ONLY.

FOR FLOWER

1. If you have already cut a flower square and set it aside while making the leaves, skip to Step 2 to begin folding. To make just the flower pattern from a coffee filter, place the flower template (F) on the filter's folded edge. Then trace around the template with a pencil, and cut out the traced pattern. (If you want to cut out the leaf patterns at the same time, see Step 1 of the leaf directions above for information on positioning it.)

2. Open the cut folded pattern out flat.

3. Position the square on point, fold it in half in the opposite direction, and unfold it. Flip the square over.

4. Keeping the square on point, fold in half from top to bottom; then unfold it.

5. Keeping the square on point, fold in half from side to side. Unfold the square. Flip the square over.

6. "Collapse" the square on the existing creases by folding the top point down to the bottom point and tucking each side in.

7. Flatten the square, and firmly crease its edges with a bone folder.

9a SWING TOP LAYER TO RIGHT.

9b FLATTEN "POCKET" FORMED.

10 REPEAT STEPS 8-9 ON OTHER FLAPS.

11 FIRMLY FOLD TIP TO STAR, AND UNFOLD. REPEAT ON OTHER SIDE.

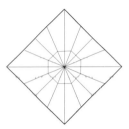

12 OPEN UP PAPER.

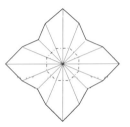

13a SINK CENTER, AND REFOLD SIDES.

13b ROTATE 180 DEGREES.

8. Fold the square's top layer to the right, like turning a page. Firmly crease the fold, and unfold it.

9. Swing the top layer to the right, opening up and squashing down the pocket it forms.

10. Firmly crease the edges of the flattened pocket, which is centered on the square. Repeat steps 8 and 9 on the three remaining flaps. After you've squashed all the flaps flat, arrange them so that there are four flaps on the right and four on the left.

11. Fold down the top point to the star in the drawing, and crease the fold extra firmly. Unfold the point; then fold it to the back, and again crease it firmly. Unfold the point.

12. Open up the paper.

13. Sink the center of the paper while refolding the sides. At first glance, this may look impossible, but think of this folded paper as a mini-umbrella. Start by pushing the center down; then pinch the edges of the center polygon. Keep working around the center until the folds take shape—practice makes for a perfect sink. What you're aiming for is to balance the flaps, with four flaps neatly tucked on the right and four on the left, between the flat "front" and "back" section. Rotate the paper 180 degrees.

14 TOP LAYER ONLY, FOLD IN TIP AND BOTTOM CORNERS.

15 REPEAT STEP 14 ON OTHER SIDES.

16 CREASE FOLDS FIRMLY.

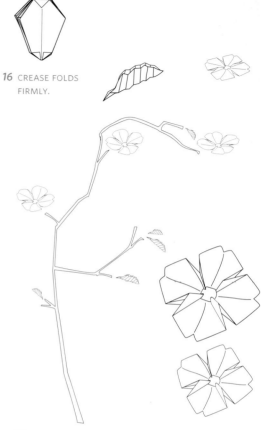

17 FOLD EDGE DOWN AND RIGHT FLAP TO LEFT. REPEAT ON OTHER SIDES.

18 TO SHAPE, PULL PETALS APART.

19 PINCH CENTER FOLDS ON PETALS' OUTER EDGES.

20 HOT-GLUE FLOWERS AND LEAVES ON REAL BRANCH.

---

14. Working with the top layer only, fold the top point down and the lower left and right corners into the center crease.

15. Repeat Step 14 on the three identical sides.

16. Crease the folds firmly.

17. Fold the edge of the first side halfway down, and also fold the right flap to the left. Repeat this step on three identical sides, again keeping four flaps on each side.

18. Slowly pull the petals apart. The center will puff up into shape.

19. Pinch the mountain folds on the center of the outer edge of the petals (so it looks like a dogwood flower).

20. Using a hot glue gun, attach the flowers and leaves to a real tree branch.

PAINTING THE FLOWERS AND LEAVES

Before you paint the flowers, practice on spare (unfolded) coffee filters. The paint bleeds VERY QUICKLY across the surface of the paper and can easily get out of control. I like to use water-color paints from a tube because they are easy to control.

Materials
Watercolor paints in white, rose
    madder (a shade of magenta),
    yellow, and green
Saucers, for mixing paint
Jar of water
Small, flat paintbrush (about a size 8)
Coffee filters, for practice
Small wooden clothespins

Flowers
On opposite sides of a saucer, squeeze a small amount of white and rose madder paint. Using a paintbrush dipped in clean water, brush the upper area of the petals (prepping the petal with water first helps the paint to bleed more evenly). Using a damp paintbrush, add the rose madder to the edge of the white paint, mixing it until you get the perfect shade. Don't add more than a drop or two of water. The less diluted the paint, the more control you will have.

With a small amount of paint on your brush, work your way around the edges of each paper flower. If you want a softer gradation of color, rub the wet painted area between your fingers. Don't worry if some of the folds fall out of the flowers when the paper gets wet. After the flowers have dried completely, you can refold and shape them as needed. For the finishing touch, dab a little yellow paint on the center of each bloom.

Leaves
Follow the folding instruction for a leaf up to Step 8 (with the leaf still accordion-folded flat). Mix the yellow and green paint in a clean saucer until you get the right shade. Add several drops of water to the paint to create a wash. Using the brush, paint an entire leaf with the watery mixture. Peek between the folds to be sure the paper is fully saturated with color, but don't worry if the paint job is uneven—unevenness looks natural. Using a small wooden clothespin, clamp the leaf so it doesn't unfold as it dries. Repeat to paint all the leaves. After the leaves have dried, open and shape them. Vary how much you open each leaf to add a natural quality to the project.

Chapter 3

CUTTING

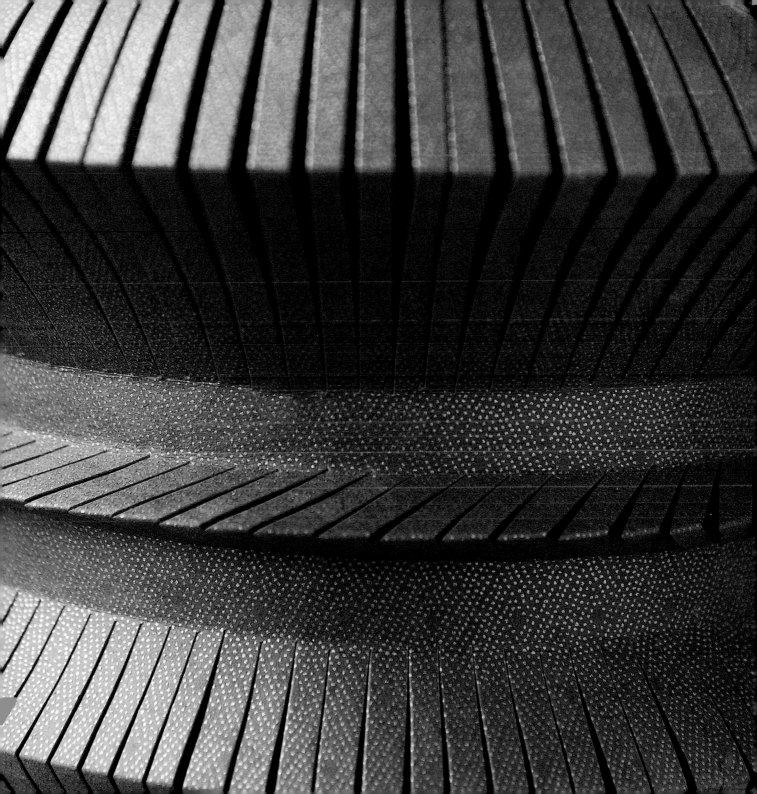

Creative people have been using scissors and other tools to decoratively cut paper for centuries. Paper cutting is be-lieved to have originated in China and from there traveled around the world. For example, in Germany and Switzerland during the 1600s, Scherenschnitte (meaning "snip with scissors") was fashionable. The delicate work, typically cut with a blade using unfolded paper, included nature scenes and flower-filled vases. Immigrants from later generations brought the tradition with them to America, where today it is carried on by the Pennsylvania Dutch. In nineteenth-century Poland, many people enjoyed wycinanki, a tradition that involves cutting detailed mirror-image designs from colored paper and layering them to decorate furniture, beams, windows, and walls. Papel picado, or punched paper, is the Mexican art of paper cutting in which layers of colored tissue paper are cut into intricate designs to make flags and banners for celebrations. In similar fashion, paper snowflakes, made from folded and cut paper, are a popular window decoration among elementary school children in the United States.

SETTING UP A WORKSPACE FOR CUTTING

For cutting down large sheets of paper or for doing multiple techniques, such as folding and cutting, you'll need a smooth, flat work surface slightly larger than the paper and cutting mat you are working with and good overhead lighting. Good lighting is important for accurate cutting and for safety. If you are cutting with scissors, a comfy chair beside a good reading lamp could prove to be an adequate workspace. Sometimes when I'm working on a project that involves multiple units, like the Garland Chain (page 66) or lots of Festive Stars (page 62) for my Christmas tree, I precut the paper to size and fold it; then later I cut out my designs while I'm relaxing in front of the television. If you do this, be careful to keep an eye on your work while actually cutting.

BEST PAPERS FOR CUTTING

All papers are suitable for cutting. Thin papers, such as copy paper and tissue paper, are easy to cut. Heavy papers, such as cold-press watercolor paper and poster board, are more difficult to cut smoothly. See Tips for Cutting Paper on page 52.

TOOLS FOR CUTTING PAPER

For more information about all of these tools, see page 17.

Scissors

You will need a variety of scissors, depending on the cutting task. An 8"-long utility scissors with a safe, blunt tip is a must-have, general-purpose scissors, good for cutting large sheets of paper into smaller sizes. I love the 5"-long Fiskars Micro-Tip scissors, whose blades are very pointed at the tip and sharp right to the very end of the blade. This makes them ideal for cutting into small spaces. A manicure scissors is a small scissors with short curved blades and my favorite tool for cutting silhouettes with small curves. Decorative paper scissors are available with blades capable of cutting shaped edges, such as scallops and wavy patterns.

X-Acto Knife and Cutting Mat

An X-Acto knife is a metal cutting tool, similar in shape and size to a pencil. It has a sharp replaceable blade at one end. When the blade becomes dull, it will not cut well, so be sure to check the blade often and replace it with a new one as necessary.

Be sure to use a self-healing cutting mat when working with an X-Acto knife, as this type of mat has a surface that remains smooth and unmarred after repeated uses. Also choose a cutting mat with a printed measurement grid. It will save time when measuring.

Steel Ruler

An 18" or 24" steel or steel-edge ruler is a good length for measuring. Use it along with an X-Acto knife to produce precise cuts.

Pencil, Eraser, and Sharpener

A pencil is the best tool for lightly tracing or marking cutting lines on paper. You can use either a regular wood pencil or a mechanical pencil. Mechanical pencils are very accurate because they are always sharp. If using a regular pencil, be sure the tip is sharpened to a point. A soft-leaded pencil works well for transferring design lines. Use an eraser, such as a Magic Rub brand eraser, for removing any unwanted marking lines, as it will remove all traces of lead without scarring the paper.

Burnishing Tools

A burnishing tool, such as a plastic "bone" folder, comes in handy for smoothing out the cut edges of the paper, which tend to bend slightly along the cut line from the force of the scissors or X-Acto knife.

Tape

Most of the time I use Scotch brand removable tape, a low-tack, repositionable, clear tape. It is especially suited for delicate papers and does not damage the finish. It works well when you want to be able to see through the tape.

Drafting tape works well for temporarily securing paper to your cutting mat. It pulls up easily from your cutting mat, as long as you don't burnish it down, and is reusable a couple of times.

CUTTING BASICS

For the projects in this book, you either cut freestyle or with a template. Freestyle cutting involves cutting out an image without marking the paper first. Cutting with a template involves cutting around a specific pattern provided.

If a project requires a template, photocopy or trace the template from the book onto copier paper and cut it out. Then position the template on your good paper, and trace around it lightly with a pencil. If you need to repeat the same design many times, try making a master template from card stock, which is more durable than copier paper. Take extra care when marking on handmade papers, as the paper surface is delicate.

Another method I use that is easy and faster than tracing around a template is to photocopy the template, tape it over the paper I plan to use, and then cut it out. This method eliminates pencil marks on your good paper, so markings don't need to be erased later.

CUTTING WITH A TEMPLATE

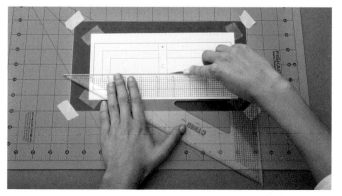

ONE EASY WAY TO CUT OUT A SHAPE IS TO PHOTOCOPY THE TEMPLATE, TAPE IT OVER YOUR PROJECT PAPER, AND THEN CUT IT OUT.

The type of cutting tool you'll need depends on the type of cutting you'll be doing. Consider whether the cuts you will be making are long or short, curved or straight, perimeter cuts, or cuts that pierce the interior of the paper.

When I cut straight lines, I prefer to use an X-Acto knife. Cutting along the edge of a steel-edge ruler with an X-Acto knife produces a cut that is very straight and accurate. For curved lines, I prefer to use scissors. Try out different options and choose what works best for you. Some people feel more comfortable with, or have more skill with, one tool or the other. As a general rule, the size of the scissors depends on the size of the job. Use scissors with long blades for longer cuts and scissors with short blades for short cuts.

Because cutting tools move differently through different kinds of paper stock, you may want to do some practice cuts with the cutting tool of your choice using a paper stock that is similar to the one you plan to use on your project. If you have extra paper for your project, practice on a scrap of the actual paper stock you plan to use.

TIPS FOR CUTTING PAPER

Most projects in this book are cut with scissors or an X-Acto knife. When cutting a single layer of paper, cut with the front, or face, up because the back side of the paper will bend slightly downward around the edges from the force of the scissors or knife during the cutting process. To smooth the cut edge on the back, or face-down side, rub a burnishing tool over it.

If it is necessary to cut multiple layers of paper, such as when cutting folded paper, it can be challenging to prevent the paper layers from shifting out of alignment. The thicker the paper stock, the more it will shift out of alignment.

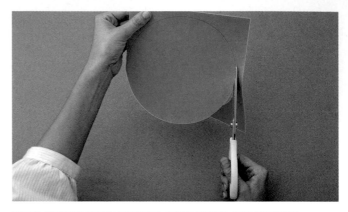

WHEN CUTTING WITH SCISSORS, MOVE PAPER, NOT SCISSORS, FEEDING PAPER WITH SWEEPING MOTION INTO BLADE.

Cutting with Scissors

Although everyone has surely used scissors before, many people do not know how to use them correctly. The best method for cutting paper is to feed the paper into the blade with a sweeping motion and make long, smooth cuts using the entire length of the blade. The key is to move the paper, not the scissors.

For straight cuts, use long-bladed scissors and insert the paper between the blades. Hold the paper firmly as you cut so it doesn't pull to one side with the force of the blades. The tip of the scissors works best for cutting sharp angles.

For tight curves, small short-bladed scissors work best. The larger the curve, the larger the blade should be. Small manicure scissors with curved blades work best on small projects with tight curves. They are a favorite tool of the silhouette artist.

When cutting out a traced shape, first roughly trim excess paper, leaving ½"-1" around the shape. Then, to cut smoothly around the shape itself, hold the scissors steady, and use your other hand to feed the paper into the blades. Cut directly on the traced line, making long smooth cuts using the entire length of the blade. If you are right-handed, start on the right side of the outline or design and cut in a counterclockwise direction. If you are left-handed, start on the left side of the outline or design and work in a clockwise direction.

WHEN CUTTING WITH X-ACTO KNIFE, LEAN WEIGHT
INTO HAND HOLDING RULER, AND DRAW KNIFE DOWN ALONG
RULER'S EDGE.

When cutting on a marked line, be careful to cut exactly on the line. Avoid over-cutting (cutting outside the line) or under-cutting (cutting inside the line) to prevent ending up with an unbalanced project. If you over-cut, you can go back and trim the excess, but the new cut never looks as smooth as a clean accurate cut on the first pass. If you under-cut and aren't happy with the result, you'll need to start over.

Cutting with an X-Acto Knife

For more control and accuracy when cutting with an X-Acto knife, stand while you cut, so you are above the project with a good view. To help prevent over- or under-cutting, avoid positions where your view is blocked by the handle of your cutting tool or positions where the cutting blade casts a shadow on your cutting path. To protect your work surface from damage, always use an X-Acto knife in combination with a cutting mat. The slightly sticky cutting surface on most mats will also help to hold the paper in place and the printed grid surface will aid in measuring.

To cut with an X-Acto knife, place your paper onto the cutting mat and position a steel straight-edge ruler in the desired position on the paper. Hold the ruler with one hand, and lean your weight onto that hand. Hold the X-Acto knife in your other hand,

and, with light pressure, draw the knife down along the edge of the ruler, but don't push the blade against the metal ruler as you cut. If you do, it will cause the ruler to slip as you move farther from the pressure points. Be careful and watch where you are cutting to avoid injury. When working with heavyweight paper stock, such as corrugated board, it is best to cut the paper halfway through on the first pass of the knife, and then make a second pass with the knife using a little more pressure, in order to cut all the way through the paper.

Always use a sharp blade in your X-Acto knife, as it will slice through the paper smoothly with little pressure. When the knife contains a dull blade, the user tends to overcompensate by adding more pressure to the blade, which transfers to the straight edge as you drag the knife through the paper. This can be very dangerous as the cutting stroke is not smooth and the added pressure against the ruler can cause it to slip. Unless you are using thick paper, the blade should easily cut the paper with one pass using light pressure. If it does not, discard the blade in an old beverage can reserved for blade disposal, and install a new blade in the X-Acto knife.

Wine-Bottle Daisy Frill

I often take a bottle of wine as a hostess gift when I visit friends and always like to make it feel special with this simple embellishment. I got the idea for it from a rather unlikely source—the paper frills that are used to decorate lamb chops and rib roasts at some restaurants. To make this frill, strips of strategically folded and cut paper are wound around the wine bottle; then the petals are opened out to create a "bloom."

SUPPLIES

Practice paper: 1 sheet of copy paper

1 sheet of 8½"-wide x 11"-long copy or specialty paper

Utility scissors

Pinking shears (optional)

Glue stick

PAPER SHOWN

I made this frill with unryu paper from Thailand.

Directions

1. Lay the paper vertically face down, fold (see Tips for Folding Paper on page 27) it in half, and then unfold it.

2. Cut (see Tips for Cutting Paper on page 52) the paper in half along the crease line.

3. Lay both paper rectangles face down, and fold each one in half, from left to right. Rotate the rectangles, so their folded edge is at the bottom.

4. Fold back both layers of the top edge of one of the folded rectangles about ½", and then unfold this edge.

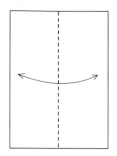

1 FOLD IN HALF, AND UNFOLD.

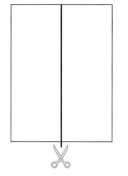

2 CUT IN HALF.

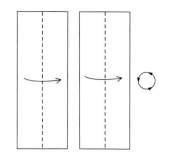

3 FOLD EACH SHEET IN HALF. ROTATE.

4a FOLD BACK BOTH EDGES.

4b UNFOLD.

5a CUT FROM FOLDED EDGE.

5b CONTINUE CUTTING. ROTATE.

6 TRIM BOTTOM OPEN EDGE USING
PINKING SHEARS.

glue

7 APPLY GLUE STICK.

5. Starting about ¼" in from the left edge, cut the paper about every ¼", stopping at the horizontal crease you made in Step 4 and ending your cuts about ¼" from the right edge. Rotate the strip, so the folded edge is at the bottom.

6. If you want to add a decorative edge to the bottom of the frill, use pinking shears to just barely trim off the strip's bottom edge. Repeat steps 4-6 for the second folded rectangle.

7. Apply a generous swipe of glue stick along the bottom (pinked) edge of each strip.

8. Position the strip's glued edge just below the top of bottle. Start winding the strip around the bottle in a gradual but tight downward spiral. Position the beginning of the second strip at the end of first one, and continue wrapping it in a tight downward spiral. For a polished finish, wrap the end of the final strip in slightly less of a downward spiral so that it ends on top of the previous round.

9. If you want to shape the frill into a "flower" and show the top of the wine bottle, gently bend the strips/ "petals" outward.

Pet Silhouette

It is amazing how the body language in a silhouette can capture an individual's character. And who better to memorialize in this way than your trusted pet. This silhouette is a snap to create with the help of a digital camera, home printer, black paper, and a pair of scissors. This silhouette technique works equally well for man or beast.

SUPPLIES
Practice paper: 1 sheet of copy paper

1 sheet of lightweight black paper, sized to accommodate photocopied pet photo

1 sheet of lightweight background paper (plain or colorful), sized to fit frame

Photo (color or black and white) of pet

Small, pointed-tip scissors

Stapler

Glue stick or spray mount

Mat and/or frame

PAPER SHOWN

I made this silhouette with colorfast art paper.

Notes: Choosing—or taking—the right photo of your pet will make this project sing. Keep in mind, first, that your pet needs to be shown with his or her body in an interesting position. Since your pet's portrait will be shown as a black silhouette on a background, it's the pet's outline that's important, while the facial features and expression will get lost in the black silhouette. So think about special details in your pet's "pose"—a floppy ear, curly tail, or unique body posture (for example, maybe your pup occasionally sleeps with legs in the air)—that will make his or her personality stand out.

Directions

1. Enlarge or reduce your pet's image on a photocopier or on your computer as needed to fit comfortably in your frame (but don't make the image so large that it fills the frame entirely; leave some space around the image to set it off on the background paper). Once you're happy with the size of your pet photo, place your photocopied photo face up on the sheet of black paper, and staple the two sheets together around the outer edges (be sure to keep the staples away from the area that will become the actual silhouette).

1 STAPLE PET PHOTO
TO BLACK PAPER.

2 CUT IN COUNTERCLOCKWISE
DIRECTION (LEFTIES CUT
CLOCKWISE).

3 PERFECT DETAILS.

4 USE GLUE TO
MOUNT SILHOUETTE.

2. Starting on the edge closest to you, cut around your pet's silhouette in a counterclockwise direction if you're right-handed or clockwise if you're a lefty. To cut a clean, smooth silhouette, rotate the paper, not the scissors—hold the scissors straight—as you cut around the image. You may want to exaggerate a few details as you cut—for example, making a few extra snips along a cat's tail or belly to give the fur some texture, or shaping a cute little nose with a bit more definition.

3. Remove the cut photo from the black background, and inspect the silhouette's details. At this point, you can snip a few thin spikes to further define the fur or again slightly exaggerate a detail to add expression, like a furrowed brow between the ears.

4. Use glue stick or spray mount to mount the black silhouette on your background paper, and then slip it into a mat or frame.

Festive Stars

This star is a fun addition to your holiday tree or Fourth of July decorations. It can also be used to add a little "twinkle" to gift boxes. To vary the shape of your stars, change the angle at which you cut the "arms" in Step 6.

FINISHED SIZE
About 8" across

SUPPLIES
Practice paper: 1 sheet of copy paper

1 sheet of lightweight specialty paper, card stock, or scrapbook paper cut to 8" wide x 10" long

Small, pointed-tip scissors

PAPERS SHOWN

I made these stars with metallic-coated card stock, scrapbook paper, and duo-printed tissue paper.

Directions

1. Position the paper vertically face down, and fold (see Tips for Folding Paper on page 27) it in half from bottom to top.

2. Roll the paper in half at the left edge, and pinch a tiny crease at the center of this edge, which will become a reference point for the next step.

3. Fold the lower right corner across to the pinch mark on the left edge.

4. Fold the right side across to align with the left folded edge (hold the paper firmly as you're matching up the edges since it tends to slip).

5. Fold the left flap across as far as it will reach.

6. Cut (see Tips for Cutting Paper on page 52) diagonally through all the layers, as shown, starting about 2" from the bottom point and cutting from right to left (to keep the folds aligned properly). The angle of the cut will determine the length of the star's arms. Turn the remaining folded triangle so that its fully folded edge is at the bottom.

7. Make a series of four parallel diagonal cuts that end about ⅜" from the top of the triangle. Finally, cut out a small wedge on the folded edge ⅜" beyond the last diagonal cut.

8. Open out the folded star flat.

9. Starting closest to the point of one of the star's arms, fold each V-shaped cut up, and then unfold it halfway. Continue folding and partly unfolding the cuts on the star's remaining arms.

Hanging tip: If you want to hang the star from a thread loop, hold a wine-bottle cork behind one of the star's points for support (to prevent creasing) as you pierce the paper with a threaded sewing needle. Then knot the thread at the desired length to make a loop.

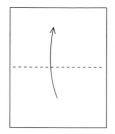

1 FOLD IN HALF.

2 PINCH LEFT EDGE
AT CENTER.

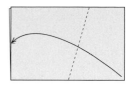

3 FOLD RIGHT CORNER
ACROSS TO PINCH.

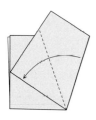

4 FOLD RIGHT
SIDE ACROSS.

5 FOLD LEFT FLAP ACROSS.

6 CUT DIAGONALLY.

7 MAKE 4 DIAGONAL
CUTS; THEN CUT WEDGE.

8 OPEN UP.

9 TO SHAPE, FOLD AND
HALFWAY UNFOLD CUTS.

Garland Chain

We all made paper chains back in elementary school. In this sophisticated, modern version of the childhood favorite, triangular links are fitted into one another without any tape or glue. I recommend scrapbook paper for this project since it's available in an endless array of colors to suit any party or decor.

FINISHED SIZE

Note: In dimensions throughout, width precedes length.

Individual link: 2" at base x 3" tall

SUPPLIES

Practice paper: 1 sheet of copy paper

One 12" square of scrapbook paper (makes 12 links for chain about 30" long)

Utility scissors

Ruler

Pencil

Glue

PAPERS SHOWN

I made these chains with an assortment of scrapbook paper and duo paper made from lokta paper and metallic-coated card stock.

Directions

1. Cut (see Tips for Cutting Paper on page 52) the 12" square of paper in half to get two 6" x 12" pieces.

2. Place one 6" x 12" piece face down, and fold (see Tips for Folding Paper on page 27) it in half vertically.

3. Measure and lightly pencil-mark the long folded edge every 2".

4. Using the pencil marks as a guide, cut the sheet into six equal parts.

5. On one of the six parts, make an angled cut from the folded edge to each corner, leaving about ¾" of the center of the folded edge intact.

6. Cut through the folded edge, and cut out the interior of the link so that it's about ⅜" wide on all sides. Hooray—you've completed your garland's first link.

   Repeat steps 5-6 on the remaining five cut parts. Then repeat steps 2-6 with the second 6" x 12" piece of paper. This will produce a total of 12 links and make a chain about 30" long.

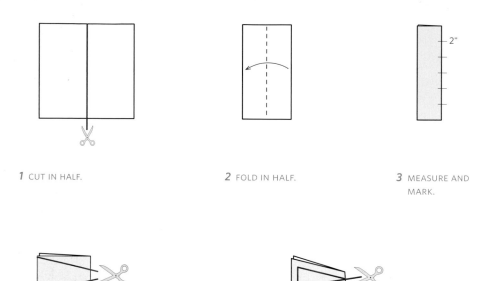

1 CUT IN HALF.

2 FOLD IN HALF.

3 MEASURE AND MARK.

4 CUT AT MARKS.

5 CUT FROM FOLDED EDGE.

6a CUT OUT INTERIOR.

6b FINISHED LINK.

7. There are two ways to connect the links to make a chain: You can add a new link (Link A) to another link (Link B) either at Link B's top folded edge or at its bottom open edge. To add Link A at Link B's top folded edge—the simpler of the two methods—first slide one of Link A's narrow folded edges, or "arms," between the layers of Link B's arms; then slip Link A into position, so Link B sits on Link A's wide base.

Adding a new link to the bottom open edge of another link is slightly more time-consuming but is useful if you want to add links of a different color or pattern to the bottom of your chain. To add a new link (Link A) this way, first open it out flat. Then slip it through the open area of the chain's bottom link (Link B), and refold Link A over Link B's base. When making chains with links of multiple colors or patterns, you may want to lay out all the links on a table or the floor to decide about color/pattern placement before beginning to connect the links.

ADDING LINKS FROM TOP EDGE

Link A

Link B

Slip link through folded edge.

Final link position.

Continue adding links.

Link B

ADDING LINKS FROM BOTTOM EDGE

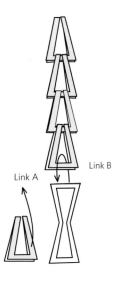

Link A

Link B

Open link up and loop over bottom link's base.

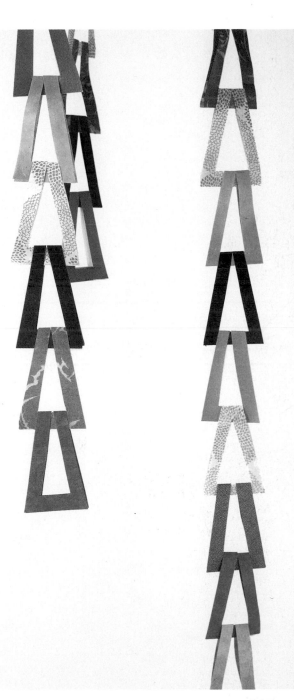

Flower Pot/ Vase Cover

This decorative cover is perfect camouflage for the typically unattractive plastic pots in which many seasonal flowering plants are sold. Simply place your pot in a two-liter soda bottle cut down to about seven inches, and place the paper cover over it. If desired, you can alter the height to fit your plant by adjusting the size of the interior panel. Short or tall, this cover is remarkably sturdy and can be reused for many seasons to come.

FINISHED SIZE

Note: In dimensions throughout, width precedes length/height.

About 8" x 7"

SUPPLIES

Practice paper: One 16" x 14" rectangle of poster board

One 16" x 14" rectangle of duo-weight specialty paper or medium-weight poster board or card stock, for vase cover

One 16" x 7" rectangle of medium-weight contrasting paper, for interior panel (optional)

Bone or wood folder

Small, pointed-tip scissors

Quick-drying white glue or adhesive dots

Small clothespin

Empty 2-liter soda bottle, for liner

PAPERS SHOWN

I made this vase with silk-screened kozo paper backed with art paper. I made this duo paper using the spray-adhesive method (see page 18).

Directions

1. Lay the paper face down, and measure and mark it along the sides, as shown in Drawing 1.

2. Starting at the top of the paper and working your way down, fold (see Tips for Folding Paper on page 27) and then unfold all the valley-fold (see page 26) lines at the marked points—at the 1" mark, 2" mark, 2½" mark, 4" mark, 4½" mark, and so on (since the paper is wide, you may find it helpful to hold a wide ruler against the marked line to get a clean fold). Next valley-fold and unfold the lines in the second part of the drawing at the following marks: 1½", 3¼", 6½", 9½", and 11½". Then turn the paper over to the other side.

3. Use the bone folder to sharply crease the lines shown in Drawing 3 as mountain folds (see page 26).

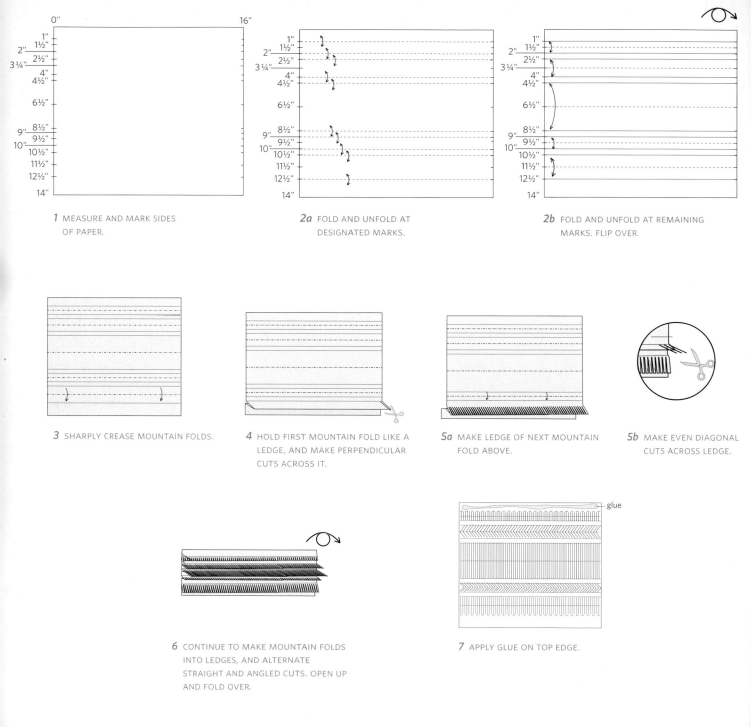

1 MEASURE AND MARK SIDES OF PAPER.

2a FOLD AND UNFOLD AT DESIGNATED MARKS.

2b FOLD AND UNFOLD AT REMAINING MARKS. FLIP OVER.

3 SHARPLY CREASE MOUNTAIN FOLDS.

4 HOLD FIRST MOUNTAIN FOLD LIKE A LEDGE, AND MAKE PERPENDICULAR CUTS ACROSS IT.

5a MAKE LEDGE OF NEXT MOUNTAIN FOLD ABOVE.

5b MAKE EVEN DIAGONAL CUTS ACROSS LEDGE.

6 CONTINUE TO MAKE MOUNTAIN FOLDS INTO LEDGES, AND ALTERNATE STRAIGHT AND ANGLED CUTS. OPEN UP AND FOLD OVER.

7 APPLY GLUE ON TOP EDGE.

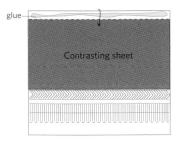

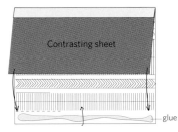

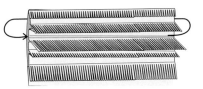

8a POSITION SHEET, AND FOLD GLUED LIP OVER.

8b GLUE BOTTOM EDGE, POSITION SHEET, AND FOLD LIP OVER.

9 SHAPE CYLINDER; GLUE ONE SIDE EDGE; TUCK TOP, BOTTOM, AND SIDE EDGES INTO ONE ANOTHER, AND CLAMP UNTIL DRY.

---

4. Starting at the bottom of the sheet, hold the first mountain fold together, like a ledge sticking out. Position the scissors perpendicular to the fold, and cut through both layers of the fold about ³⁄₁₆" from the right edge, cutting up to but not over the crease lines at the base of the ledge. Move the paper (not the scissors) over about ³⁄₁₆" to the right, and again cut through both layers of the fold. Continue holding the scissors steady, moving the paper, and making quick, straight parallel cuts through the fold along the length of the ledge.

5. Move up to the next mountain fold, and hold it together, as before, like a ledge. On this row, your goal is to make diagonal cuts, so hold your scissors at a 45-degree angle to the ledge, and snip through both layers about ³⁄₁₆" from the right edge up to but not over the crease lines at the base of the ledge. Holding the scissors steady at the same angle, move the paper ³⁄₁₆" to the right, and

make another cut as before. Continue making quick, parallel diagonal cuts across the length of the ledge, moving the paper while keeping the scissors steady.

6. Continue to move up and work with each of the three remaining mountain folds, holding each one as a ledge, and cutting across its length. Alternate the angle of the cuts on each ledge, so they're perpendicular on the center and top and bottom ledges and diagonal on the ledges in between. Then flip the paper over so that it's face down.

7. With the paper somewhat flattened out, spread glue on the edge of the top lip.

8. If you want to have a contrasting sheet of paper inside the vase cover, now's the time to position its top edge at the base of the vase cover's top fold (if you don't want to add the contrasting interior paper, go to Step 9 now). Then fold down the

vase cover's glued top lip over the contrasting paper.

Next spread glue on the vase cover's bottom lip, tuck in the bottom edge of the contrasting paper at the vase cover's bottom fold, and fold the lip up in place over the contrasting paper.

9. Before gluing the vase cover's side edges together, shape the paper into a cylinder, and test-fit the two edges together. Then apply glue or adhesive dots to one of the vase cover's side edges, fold the cover again into a cylinder, tuck the top and bottom edges into one another, and use a small clothespin to hold the edges in place until the glue dries.

Cut off the top of the soda bottle so that the bottle fits neatly inside the vase cover, and slip the cover over it.

Holiday Ornaments

These geometric ornaments are relatively quick to make and look modern and beautiful on a Christmas tree—or wherever you want to elicit some holiday cheer. Try them with textured or metallic paper, too—or maybe sprinkle with a little glitter. Because they're durable and flatten for easy storage, they can be reused from year to year.

FINISHED SIZE
3" wide x 6" long

SUPPLIES
Practice paper: One 12" square of scrapbook paper

One 12"square of medium-weight scrapbook paper, card stock, or specialty paper cut into four 6" squares (yields 8 ornaments)

Small, pointed-tip scissors

⅛"-round paper punch

String or thread

PAPERS SHOWN

I made these ornaments with an assortment of iridescent coated card stock and duo-printed metallic lokta paper.

Directions

1. Position one 6" square of paper face up, and fold (see Tips for Folding Paper on page 27) it in half, from top to bottom.

2. Fold the top sheet in half, and flip the paper over to the other side.

3. Fold the top sheet in half.

4. Fold the paper in half along the top edge, and pinch a tiny crease at the center, which will become a reference point in the following step.

5. Cut (see Tips for Cutting Paper on page 52) through all layers from each bottom corner to the pinched center crease on the top edge, which will produce—hooray!—identical-twin folded triangles. Set one triangle aside to make another ornament later.

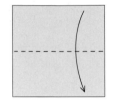

1 FOLD IN HALF.

2a FOLD TOP SHEET IN HALF.

2b FLIP OVER.

3 FOLD TOP SHEET IN HALF.

4 PINCH FOLD
EDGE AT CENTER.

5a CUT THROUGH ALL LAYERS.

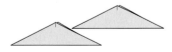

5b SEPARATE UNITS.

6 CUT ON FOLDED EDGE.

7 CONTINUE CUTTING FOLDED EDGE;
THEN CUT WEDGES.

8 FOLD AND UNFOLD.

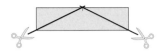

9 OPEN OUT. ROTATE.

10 ALTERNATE PUSHING FLAPS
FORWARD AND BACKWARD.

6. Starting from the triangle's bottom folded edge, cut two parallel lines about ¼" on either side of the center pinch mark, stopping your cutting lines about ¼" from the triangle's top edge.

7. Make three more parallel cuts about ¼" apart on each side of the two center cuts, again stopping about ¼" from the triangle's top edge. Finally, cut a wedge at each end, cutting its top angled edge about ¼" from the triangle's top edge.

8. Fold up the parallel cuts at their top edge, and then unfold them.

9. Open out the folded triangle flat and rotate the flat diamond 90 degrees.

10. Alternate popping the cut flaps forward and backward to make the ornament three-dimensional. Use a small paper punch to make a hole near the top of the ornament, and thread it with string or thread to hang the ornament. Alternatively, skip the hole, and run the string or thread through the top opening on the ornament.

Repeat steps 6-10 with the second triangle you set aside to make another ornament.

Op Art Mobile

The geometric mobiles here and on page 83 look as though they're made out of many concentric units but each square or rectangle is actually made from one strategically cut and folded piece of paper. To emphasize the optical illusion, try making the mobile in contrasting duo paper. The three-unit, vertical mobile here is easier to make than the larger six-unit on page 83, which requires balancing.

FINISHED SIZE

Note: In dimensions throughout, width precedes length.

Large mobile (page 83): About 38" x 17"

Small mobile (at left): About 7" x 15"

SUPPLIES

Practice paper: One 12" square of scrapbook paper

One 12" x 24" sheet of card stock or three 12" squares of scrapbook paper (makes 1 large mobile; for duo paper [see page 14] mobile, double amount of paper)

Photocopied patterns (see Step 1) or three sheets of 8½" x 11" graph paper, with four squares per inch

PAPERS SHOWN

I made this mobile with metallic-coated card stock and printed vellum.

Spray adhesive, for making duo paper (optional)

Masking tape

Cutting mat

Removable tape

Steel ruler

Pencil

Scoring tool (see page 19)

X-Acto knife

Utility scissors

Hand-sewing needle and black thread

Four 18" lengths of 18-gauge floral wire (only for large mobile)

Wire cutters (only for large mobile)

Needle-nose pliers (only for large mobile)

Clear nail polish or Super Glue (only for large mobile)

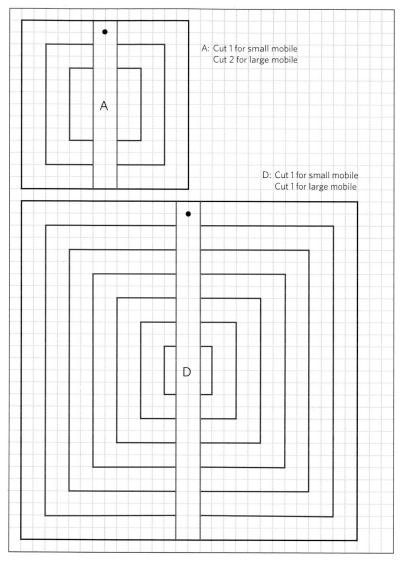

A: Cut 1 for small mobile
Cut 2 for large mobile

D: Cut 1 for small mobile
Cut 1 for large mobile

Directions

Notes: The directions here are for making the large, six-piece mobile. If you want to start with a smaller, easier mobile, prepare just parts A, B, and D, and hang them in a vertical line (see the diagram on page 82).

If you want to use duo paper for the mobile, follow the directions on page 14 to prepare the paper in advance.

1. First, using a color photocopier and enlarging the patterns 200%, photocopy the diagrams for parts

A and B twice, and make a single photocopy of parts C and D. Cut out the photocopies, leaving about a 1" border all around each diagram.

2. Use masking tape to tape your card stock (or paper) to your cutting mat at all four corners. Position the first photocopied diagram on the taped card stock, about 1" in from its edges, and use removable tape to tape down all the diagram's borders. (If you don't have access to a photocopier, you can easily duplicate the diagrams on graph paper since the originals are shown set up on gridded paper. Just position the graph paper on the card stock about 1" from its edges, and secure it with removable tape on all sides. Then make your cutting grid by measuring and pencil-marking the graph paper just like the original diagram.) After taping the diagram in place, score (see page 88) the two blue center lines that run through it.

3. With the pattern still taped in place, carefully follow the pattern to cut (see Tips for Cutting Paper on page 52) the design's concentric rectangles or squares by starting at the two blue lines at the center and cutting away from them along all the horizontal red lines (be sure not to cut through the center blue lines). Then cut along all the vertical red lines. Finally cut out the diagram's outside black edge, and remove the

pattern. Depending on the thickness of your card stock, it may take two passes to make each cut through it.

Repeat steps 2-3 to prepare and cut out all the parts for either the large or small mobile.

4. To prepare the large mobile's parts for hanging, use a needle threaded with a single strand of black thread about 12" long, and sew through the top center point (shown as a black dot on the pattern, about ¼" from the top edge) of parts A, B, and C. Then tie off the thread on each part, so the knot sits at its top center edge, and leave the long thread tail uncut for now. Then sew a 15" length of thread at the top center of Part D, and similarly tie it off. (If you're making the three-part mobile, likewise sew and tie off a 12"-long thread to the top center edge of parts A and D, and then sew a 3-ft.-to 4-ft.-long thread for hanging the completed mobile to the top center edge of Part B.)

FOR LARGE MOBILE ONLY

5. Next prepare the wire "arms" from which you'll suspend the mobile's parts by measuring and cutting the four 18"-long floral wires to the following lengths: 6", 9", 12", 15", and 18" (note that cutting the 6" length also gives you the 12" length).

6. Using the needle-nose pliers, make a loop at both ends of each length of wire. Be sure that both loops are identical and lie in the same plane.

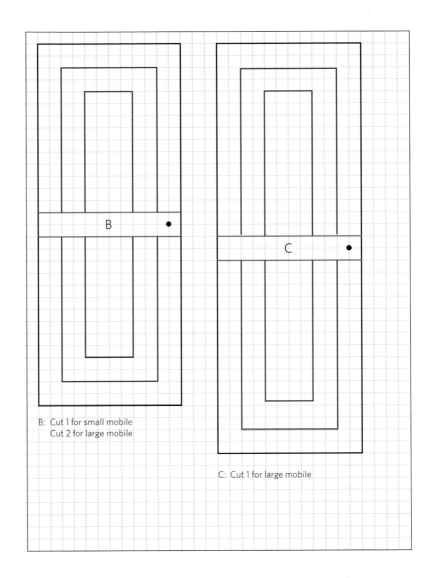

B: Cut 1 for small mobile
Cut 2 for large mobile

C: Cut 1 for large mobile

7. You'll assemble the mobile, one suspended part at a time, balancing each of the mobile's sections as you work your way up from the bottom. Begin by suspending one Part A from each end of the 6" wire, so the parts hang about 1" below the wire, as shown in the diagram on page 82.

Wrap the thread around each end of the wire a few times, tie off the thread, and cut off the excess. Then tie a 10"-long thread to the center of the wire, and set the part aside while you prepare what will be the next section above it.

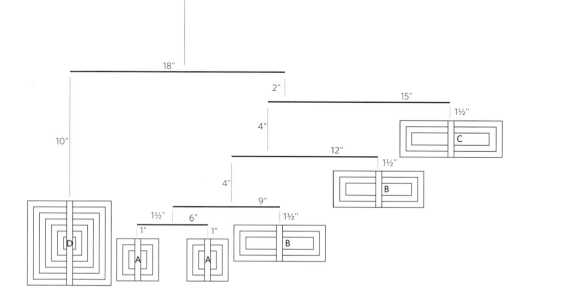

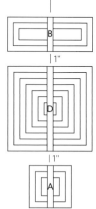

8. Suspend one Part B from one end of the 9" wire, and tie a 10"-long thread to the center of that wire. Now connect the other end of the 9" wire to the center thread on the first (6"-wire) suspended section, tying the thread so it's about 1½" long, as shown in the diagram above. (Note that you'll use the same diagram throughout as a reference for suspending the remaining parts, and that the distance suggested for hanging the parts below the wire is variable and not related to balancing the parts but rather to enabling them to pivot freely in the completed mobile.)

9. Now you need to balance the two sections you've just made. Think of this balancing process like finding your weight on a doctor's scale: You'll find the balancing point on each arm by slowly nudging the knotted thread at the center of the wire to the left or right to counterbalance the suspended parts below that point. After establishing the balancing point, add a drop of clear nail polish or glue to the knot at the center of the wire to secure it.

10. Next suspend the second Part B from one end of the 12" wire, and tie a 10"-long thread at the center of the wire. Then connect this section to the center thread of the 9"-wire section below it, and balance the newly added section, as before.

I USED THE SPRAY ADHESIVE METHOD TO CREATE DUO PAPER
(SEE PAGE 14) FOR THIS MOBILE FROM TWO SHEETS OF PRINTED
AND EMBOSSED FAUX WOOD PAPER.

11. Suspend Part C from one end of the 15" wire, and repeat the process to attach and balance it to the 12" wire below it. Finally suspend Part D from one end of the 18" wire, and repeat the process to attach and balance it to the 15" wire, adding a 3-ft-. to 4-ft.-long thread at the center of the wire for hanging the complete mobile.

FOR LARGE AND SMALL MOBILES

12. After hanging the mobile, finish it by folding the alternate concentric squares or rectangles of each part as follows: Leave the smallest center square/rectangle flat and unfolded. On the next square/rectangle out, fold the right half of the square/rectangle to the front and the left half to the back, effectively rotating the two halves of this square/rectangle so that they sit at a right angle to the unfolded center square/rectangle. Leave the next square/rectangle flat and unfolded. On the next square/rectangle out, again fold the right half of the square/rectangle to the front and the left half to the back. Continue folding the squares/rectangles this way, leaving every other one flat and unfolded, and folding the right half of the alternate squares/rectangles to the front and the left half to the back. While the folding process is very simple, the results look complicated and give the illusion of the squares/rectangles bisecting one another.

Chapter 4

SCORING AND SCULPTING

Scoring is used as a pre-folding step. A blunt scoring tool is run along a line to help break down the paper fibers and then the paper is folded along the scored line. Scoring stiff papers, such as card stock, helps produce clean folds and prevents cracks on both sides of the folded edge. There is no need to score thin flexible paper, as it can be folded neatly and easily without scoring.

Papers are folded along scored lines to create dimensional pieces. If you've never scored and sculpted paper before, set aside an hour or so, as this process can be addictive. It is amazing how the paper can be shaped in your hands and how easily the paper retains the shape.

The templates provided for the projects are intended to be used as guides for cutting out the shaped units. The scoring can all be done freehand, or you can use a ruler along with your scoring tool for straight sections of a scored line. All the projects in this book allow for personal flair, so if your scoring isn't identical to mine, don't worry—the result will be slightly different, but that's what gives each piece character.

SETTING UP A WORKSPACE FOR SCORING

To score paper, you'll need a smooth, flat work surface large enough to comfortably rotate your paper. Good lighting is essential to see the scored lines; if you have difficulty seeing them, tilt the paper slightly. Sometimes changing the angle of the paper under the light will make the scored lines more visible.

BEST PAPERS FOR SCORING

Card stock or similar-weight scrapbook paper is the perfect weight with which to start experimenting. After you've practiced bending scored card stock into shape, you can move onto cold-press watercolor paper, which is a bit more expensive. A benefit of cold-press watercolor paper is that, when shaping a tight curve, the paper's texture hides stress wrinkles that sometimes radiate from the scored line.

For more information about all of these tools, see pages 17-21.

Scoring Tool

It is important to use a scoring tool that is comfortable in your hand, since you will be pressing on it firmly. An uncomfortable grip will soon cause finger fatigue and frustration. One of the most common tools for scoring paper is the pointed tip of a bone folder, although sometimes I find this tool too clunky. Generally, I like to use an antique fish knife or, if the paper is delicate, one of my many wooden clay-sculpting tools. The fish knife has a thin, wide blade that is as dull as a butter knife and has a comfortable handle. The wooden clay-sculpting tools are so smooth they rarely scratch the paper. Plastic tools usually have a seam, which can sometimes scratch the paper's surface, especially if you are working with a delicate paper.

There are some scoring tools on the market for making straight score lines. These are mainly intended for making greeting cards, envelopes, and boxes but can also be used for making accordion folds.

Scoring Mat

To produce good scored lines, it is helpful to have a surface that has a bit of give under your paper, so when you apply pressure to the paper, it has a surface to sink into. A cork board makes a great scoring mat. I typically use an inexpensive 6" x 9" cork trivet and it works wonderfully for scoring smaller projects. A thick pad of newsprint will also work well.

Pencil, Eraser, and Sharpener

A sharp pencil is handy for lightly marking precise scored lines. I use a Magic Rub brand eraser for erasing unwanted lines. It works well for removing marks without marring the surface of the paper.

Steel Ruler

A steel-edge ruler is used along with a scoring tool, such as a bone folder, to create straight scored lines.

For best results, always make test scored lines on the same paper stock that you plan to use on the final project, so you can get a feel for how much pressure is needed to score a clean, thin line. Each paper may require a different amount of pressure. With this process, practice makes perfect.

Place your paper on your scoring surface, such as a cork board. Using a dull, pointed scoring tool, press firmly while dragging the tool's narrow edge over the surface of the paper. The result of this action is a thin, depressed "scar," or scored line. To prevent cutting through the paper, be sure to use a dull scoring tool and paper that is not brittle.

WHEN SCORING STRAIGHT LINES WITH METAL RULER, DRAG TOOL ALONG EDGE OF RULER. SCORE SAME LINE MORE THAN ONCE, IF NECESSARY.

FOLD AWAY FROM SCORED LINES ON EACH SIDE OF SCORE.

SCORING AND FOLDING STRAIGHT LINES

Scoring

On straight lines, such as for the spine of a card, drag the scoring tool along the edge of a ruler. A few passes may be necessary to score the paper.

Folding

On straight scored lines, fold along the scored line away from the score, gently pinching the line's edge into shape. (For example, when scoring the spine of a greeting card, the scored line will be on the exterior of the card, with the raised score itself on the inside of the card.) Then burnish the edge with a burnishing tool, such as a bone folder. To burnish, draw the narrow, flat edge of the tool across the fold line with even pressure to sharply crease the line. Do not over-burnish, especially with brittle paper, such as vellum, because the paper could split open along the fold.

SCORE CURVED LINES GENTLY AND IN ONE PASS.

BEGIN FOLDING CURVED LINES ON STRAIGHTEST SECTION OF CURVE, SLOWLY BENDING AND PINCHING ALONG FOLD AND MOVING INTO CURVE.

SCORING AND FOLDING CURVED LINES

Scoring

On curved lines, do not press the scoring tool too firmly, as it will be difficult to drag your tool smoothly over the surface. You should only make one pass with the scoring tool on curves, as it is very difficult to retrace your scored path accurately.

Folding

On curved lines, begin folding on the straightest section of the scored line, slowly bending and pinching along the fold and moving into the curve. Tight curves can be coiled inward a bit and the folded edge pinched to reinforce the shape. You may want to go back and pinch along the shape again to reinforce it. For practice, start with simple crescent-shaped curves. When you get comfortable scoring and folding crescent shaped curves, move on to S curves.

FOLDING MULTIPLE SCORED LINES

On units with more than one scored line, first shape the center or longest scored line. Then move to one side of the center (or longest) line, and shape each of the scored lines on that side, working from the center line outward. Finally, move to the other side of the center line, and repeat the process.

WHEN FOLDING MULTIPLE SCORED LINES, START WITH CENTER OR LONGEST SCORED LINE. THEN FOLD ALL SCORES ON ONE SIDE OF STARTING POINT, WORKING FROM CENTER OUT; REPEAT ON OTHER SIDE.

A-Little-Bird-Told-Me Greeting Card (& Envelope)

Have you heard some good news and want to pass it along? Is a friend getting hitched or having a baby? Here's a sweet greeting card to spread the word. It's cut, scored, and folded—and quicker to make than a trip to the card store. Make an accompanying envelope out of the prettiest decorative paper you can find, or stick with a standard business-sized envelope. The card will fit into either.

FINISHED SIZE

Note: In dimensions throughout, width precedes length.

Folded card: 4" x 9"

SUPPLIES

Practice paper: 1 sheet of lightweight scrapbook or construction paper

One 4" x 6" rectangle of lightweight, chartreuse card stock or scrapbook or construction paper, for birds

One 4" x 9" rectangle of grey card stock or scrapbook paper, for branch and eyes.

PAPERS SHOWN

I used scrapbook paper for the birds and branch, card stock for the card, and silkscreened chiyogami paper from Japan for the envelope.

One 8" x 9" rectangle of medium-weight white card stock, for card

One 12" x 10" rectangle of decorative paper, for envelope (or use standard business envelope)

Photocopied patterns (see Step 1)

Utility scissors

Removable tape

Scoring tool and mat (see page 87)

⅛"-round paper punch, for bird eyes

Bone or wood folder

Adhesive dots and double-sided tape

Pinking shears

Glue stick, for envelope

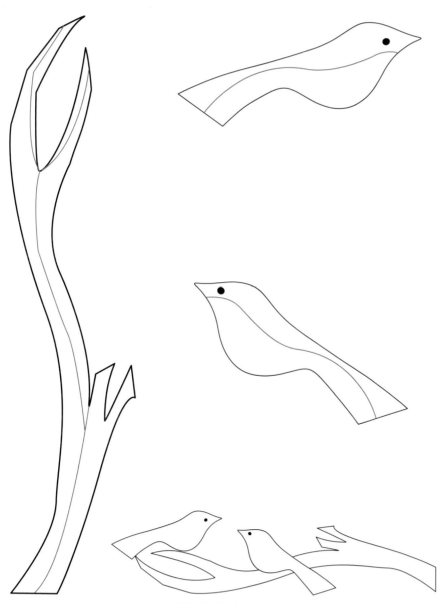

Position birds as above or as you like.

Directions

1. Photocopy the bird and branch patterns, enlarging them by 150%. Trim around each pattern, leaving a generous ½" border for taping the pattern to your card stock or paper. (You may want to make a couple extra birds to add a bit of color inside the card, or to embellish the envelope.) Using removable tape, attach the borders of the branch pattern and the two bird patterns to the paper you've chosen for each element.

2. Score (see Tips for Scoring Paper on page 87) the paper along each bird's center line. Cut out the birds (see Tips for Cutting Paper on page 52), and remove the photocopied patterns.

3. With the scored side of one bird facing up, start folding (see Tips for Folding Paper on page 27) the paper away from the scored line on each side, which will cause the bird's tail to curl downward and its body slightly upward. Smooth out any stress wrinkles you find radiating from the folded scored line by pinching the folded line between your fingers to coax it into shape, which will reduce the stress on the surrounding paper (note that the lighter the paper, the fewer wrinkles you'll have). Repeat this step with the remaining cut and scored birds.

MAKING YOUR OWN ENVELOPE

To create a custom envelope, enlarge the template given at right by 465% and follow the instructions provided.

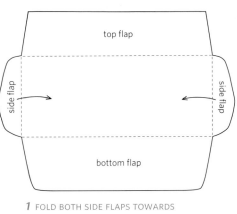

1 FOLD BOTH SIDE FLAPS TOWARDS EACH OTHER.

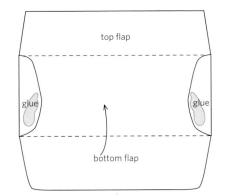

2 APPLY A SWIPE OF GLUE STICK ON LOWER HALF OF SIDE FLAPS. FOLD BOTTOM FLAP UP TOWARDS CENTER.

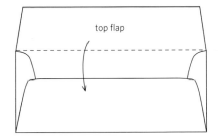

3a FOLD TOP FLAP DOWN TOWARDS CENTER.

3b COMPLETED ENVELOPE.

4. Score the center lines of the branch, cut out the branch, and remove the pattern.

5. Using a scrap of the grey branch paper, punch out an eye for each birdie—I suggest making a few extra since they go missing with the slightest breeze!

6. Fold the white card stock in half to make a 4" x 9" card base, and firmly press the crease with the bone folder.

7. Arrange the elements on the card, and use adhesive dots or double-sided tape along the lowest points of the shaped edge to attach the bird and branch to the card's surface.

8. Use a tiny adhesive dot to attach an eye to each bird.

9. Whether you make your own envelope, using the diagrams above, or use a standard business envelope, dress it up with an extra birdie and a colored address label cut out with pinking shears.

Scored Heart, Good News Trumpet, Flower, Swirl, Snake, and Exclamation Point!

These graceful little doodads are excellent decorations to use when making a card or wrapping a gift. Customize the size to your needs by enlarging or reducing the patterns given, then simply adhere them with adhesive dots or double-sided tape. They are best made from card stock or scrapbook paper, so they hold their shape. These are great to make from scraps saved from other projects. Shown at left are the exclamation point, flowers, snake, half of a heart, and a trumpet.

SUPPLIES

FOR ALL MOTIFS
Practice paper: 1 sheet of scrapbook paper

1 piece of medium-weight card stock or scrapbook paper about 1" larger on all sides than the motif you're making

Photocopied pattern (see Step 1)

Small, pointed-tip scissors

Removable tape

Scoring tool and mat (see page 87)

Adhesive dots or double-sided tape

Pencil and eraser, for snake only

FOR FLOWER
Compass

White tacky glue

PAPERS SHOWN

I made all of these doodads with scrapbook paper.

Directions

FOR TRUMPET, HEART, SWIRL STEM, AND EXCLAMATION POINT

1. Photocopy the patterns, enlarging or reducing them as desired, and cut them out with a generous ½" border around each motif.

2. Using removable tape, tape the borders of the patterns to the card stock or scrapbook paper, and cut out (see page 52) the motifs along the pattern lines. Examine the cut edges, and trim off any rough areas to smooth them out.

3. Using your scoring tool, slowly score (see Tips for Scoring Paper on page 87) the center line on each motif using line on pattern.

4. To fold a motif into a three-dimensional shape, first place it with the scored side facing up. Then find the scored line's longest straight section, and begin folding there, working your way into any of the scored line's tight curves. As you work, gently and slowly fold the paper away from the scored line on each side, one section at a time. When folding a curved scored line, you may find it helpful to hold your scoring tool beneath the paper and bend the scored line over it. You can also try holding one edge of the paper in

GOOD NEWS TRUMPET

HEART
(USE TWO HALVES TOGETHER TO
CREATE HEART OR SEPARATELY AS
DECORATIVE SWIRLS)

SWIRL STEM
(NOT SHOWN)

EXCLAMATION POINT

each hand and gently pushing the two edges together to put pressure on the scored line and bend the paper on each side of it. The key is to work slowly and gently and to keep reinforcing the fold line you're making; gradually the paper will take three-dimensional shape. Smooth out any stress wrinkles you find radiating from the folded scored line by pinching the folded line between your fingers to coax it into shape (and reduce the stress on the surrounding paper). Repeat this step on the remaining cut motifs.

5. Arrange the motifs on a card, gift box, or another object that you're embellishing, and use adhesive dots or double-sided tape along the lowest points of the shaped edges to attach them to the surface.

FOR FLOWER

1. Using your compass, draw a 4½"-diameter circle on the card stock or scrapbook paper. Then, using the same center point, draw two more concentric circles, one 2¼" in diameter and a second one 1½" in diameter.

2. Cut out the 4½"-diameter circle. Then make a straight cut from the outer edge to the pinhole center made by your compass.

Next score the two center rings by positioning a shot glass or another round object the right size over one ring at a time, and scoring around the glass or object with your scoring tool (I like to use a compass with a metal scoring rod inserted).

To make the flower become three-dimensional, start folding the paper on either side of the center-circle scored line up away from the line

FLOWER

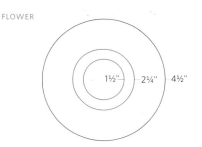

1 DRAW CIRCLES WITH COMPASS.

2 CUT PERIMETER, AND CUT SLIT TO CENTER.
SCORE TWO CENTER CIRCLES.

3 OVERLAP, AND GLUE
IN POSITION.

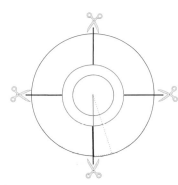

4 CUT TO FIRST SCORED CIRCLE.

5 FOR EQUIDISTANT PETALS, CUT EACH QUARTER IN HALF AND
THEN IN HALF AGAIN. TRIM PETAL CORNERS DIAGONALLY.

(which will produce a slight cone shape when you overlap the cut edges in the next step). Then bend the paper on the outside edge of the neighboring scored circle down in the opposite direction.

3. Slightly overlap the circle's cut edges, right side over left, by about ½", and see if you like the shape produced. If not, increase or reduce the overlap to your liking. Then use white tacky glue to glue the overlapped edges neatly together (holding them at the outer edge with a binder clip or clothes pin helps keep them in place until the glue sets).

4. To cut the flower's petals evenly, first position the overlapped seam at what would be six o'clock on a clock face, and cut from the outer edge up to the first concentric circle. Then cut a straight line from the outer edge to the first circle directly opposite at twelve o'clock, and repeat this cut at three o'clock and nine o'clock. Working your way around the circle, cut each section in half again, cutting from the outer edge up to the first circle; then cut the two resulting sections in half again. In the end, you'll have made 16 equal petals.

5. Finally shape the ends of each petal by snipping the corners off at an angle. And, as with the other motifs above, attach the flower to your card or gift box with adhesive dots or double-sided tape along the lowest points of the shaped edge to adhere it to the surface.

FOR SNAKE

1. Follow the instructions on page 99, placing the outline closer to the loopy line in Step 3 to make a smaller doodad-sized snake.

Snakes, Snakes, Snakes, and More Scored Snakes

A slithering snake is the inspiration for this amazingly easy-to-make abstract wall art. Cut, score, and sculpt a few different snakes, and then frame one or more of your favorites. Guys are really intrigued by this project. If you're looking to charm one, this no-fuss project is a good place to *ssssstart*.

FINISHED SIZE

Note: In dimensions throughout, height precedes the width.

20" x 16"

SUPPLIES

Practice paper: 1 sheet of poster board

One 20" x 30" sheet of medium-weight black card stock (makes 2 snakes)

One 20" x 16" rectangle of poster or mat board, for background

Utility scissors

Soft-leaded pencil

Scoring tool and mat (see page 87)

Eraser

Adhesive dots or double-sided tape

One 20" x 16" frame

PAPER SHOWN

I used 140lb. card stock to make these snakes.

Directions

1. Position the card stock horizontally and face up, and cut (see Tips for Cutting Paper on page 52) it in half to make two 20" x 15" sheets. Repeat the steps below on both sheets.

2. Using a pencil, loosely draw a loopy line down the center of the paper (see Drawing 2 on page 100). Don't worry if your drawing doesn't look exactly like the one pictured. As my friend Toby says, "In nature, all snakes in the forest are different."

3. Lightly draw an outline shape around your loopy line about ¾" wide on each side of the line, exaggerating the shape around the loops. Draw freely as you sketch the snake's head; you can fine-tune it later when cutting it out.

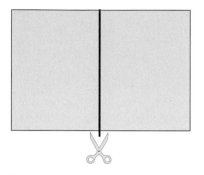

1 CUT PAPER IN HALF.

2 DRAW LOOPY LINE.

3 DRAW OUTLINE SHAPE
AROUND LOOPY LINE.

4. Using your scoring tool, slowly score (see Tips for Scoring Paper on page 87) the center line. Just before you get to the snake's head, split your scored line to make a Y to help shape the head.

5. Cut out the snake, examine the cut edges, and trim off any rough areas to smooth them out. Erase all the remaining pencil marks.

6. To fold the card stock along the scored line and manipulate the snake into shape, first position the paper with the scored side up. Then find one of the scored line's longest straight sections, and begin folding there, working your way from the straight section into the scored line's tight curves. As you work, gently and slowly fold the paper away from the scored line on each side, one section at a time. When folding a curved section of the scored line, you may find it helpful to hold your scoring tool beneath the paper and bend the scored line over it. You can also try holding one edge of the paper in each hand and gently pushing the two edges together to put pressure on the scored line and bend the paper on each side of it. The key is to work slowly and gently and to keep

 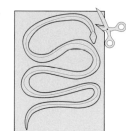

4 SCORE CENTER LINE, SPLITTING LINE AT BASE OF HEAD TO MAKE A Y.

5 CUT OUT SNAKE.

6 SCULPT SNAKE BY FOLDING EDGES BACK FROM SCORED LINE.

reinforcing the fold line you're making; gradually the paper will take three-dimensional shape. Smooth out any stress wrinkles you find radiating from the folded scored line by pinching the folded line between your fingers to coax it into shape (and reduce the stress on the surrounding paper).

7. Arrange the completed snake(s) on the poster or mat board, and use adhesive dots or double-sided tape along the lowest points of the shaped edges to attach them to the board. Now pop the matted snakes into your frame.

Baroque Mirror Frame

Inspired by the decorative arts of Louis XIV, this frame will add a bit of grandeur to your living room or front hall. The scroll-like pieces are cut, scored, and sculpted from stiff watercolor paper to mimic the plaster moldings of France.

FINISHED SIZE
25½" wide x 28" long

SUPPLIES
Practice paper: 1 sheet of card stock

Three 12"-wide x 18"-long sheets of heavyweight, cold-press watercolor paper

Photocopied patterns (see Step 1)

Small, pointed-tip scissors

Removable tape

Scoring tool and mat (see page 87)

1 frame (wood or metal), 25½" wide x 28" long, with 3"-wide molding

Archival craft putty (see page 20) or hot glue gun

PAPER SHOWN
I made this frame with 140lb. cold-press watercolor paper.

Notes: If your frame is a different size than that suggested here, adjust the size of the pattern's corner elements (B1 and B2), so each of their sides is about one-quarter the length of the side of the frame on which they sit.

Watercolor paper comes in cold-press and hot-press forms. Cold-press paper has a rougher surface, which will hide any folding imperfections far better than its smooth-surfaced hot-press counterpart.

6a POSITION CORNER UNITS FIRST; THEN CENTER FLEUR-DE-LIS.

6b PLACE REMAINING UNITS (NOTE OVERLAPPING EDGES AND SYMMETRY).

Directions

1. Photocopy the patterns for the decorative elements, enlarging them 400% (or as explained in the Note on page 103 if your frame size differs from that suggested in Supplies) and cutting them out with a 1" border around them. Using removable tape, tape down each pattern on the watercolor paper.

2. Cut out all the decorative elements (see Tips for Cutting Paper on page 52). Then examine the cut edges, and trim off any rough areas to smooth them out.

3. To get a feel for scoring (see Tips for Scoring Paper on page 87) and folding a scored line, start with the simplest element—one of the two mirror-image bottom-center pieces (E). Using your scoring tool, trace the curved path of the pattern's line.

4. To fold the stiff watercolor paper along the scored line and manipulate the element into shape, first position the paper with the scored side up. Then find the scored line's longest straight section, and begin folding there, working your way into any of the scored line's tight curves. As you work, gently and slowly fold the paper away from the scored line on each side, one section at a time. When folding a curved scored line, you may find it helpful to hold your scoring tool beneath the paper and bend the scored line over it. You can also try holding one edge of the paper in each hand and gently pushing the two edges together to put pressure on the scored line and bend the paper on each side of it. The key is to work slowly and gently and to keep reinforcing the fold line you're making; gradually the paper will take three-dimensional shape. Smooth out any stress wrinkles you find radiating from the folded scored line by pinching the folded line between your fingers to coax it into shape (and reduce the stress on the surrounding paper).

5. Repeat steps 3-4 with all the remaining cut-out elements. Note that all these remaining elements have multiple scored lines. To work with multiple scored lines, start with the center scored line and bend the paper away from the scored line on each side. Next move to the adjacent scored line on one side, and fold the paper in the opposite direction from the neighboring center fold. Then work your way across the remaining scored lines on that same side, alternating the direction in which you fold the paper. Repeat the process on the other side of the center scored line.

6. If your frame is not new, be sure to clean and dry its surface before affixing the decorative elements. Then arrange the elements on the frame, slightly overlapping them, as shown in drawings 6a and 6b: Start by positioning the corner elements (B1 and B2). Next place the top-center fleur-de-lis (A). Then add the remaining elements (C, D, and E), positioning them evenly side-to-side and top-to-bottom along the frame's edges. To fine-tune your layout, you'll find craft putty helpful since it enables you to reposition the elements as you work and then hardens over time (hot glue is a less expensive alternative to craft putty, but I prefer craft putty since it's not as messy to work with).

Chapter 5

PLEATING

Pleating is one of my favorite folding techniques. I enjoy the process, and I love the look! There are many pleating techniques; however, in this book I've only included accordion and knife pleats. Accordion pleats resemble the bellows of an accordion; the pleats are exactly the same width and fold back and forth on top of one another. Knife pleats are folded at regular intervals but alternate in width, causing them to overlap. This style of pleating is commonly found in clothing—a good example can be seen in traditional Scottish kilts.

SETTING UP A WORKSPACE FOR PLEATING

To create pleats in paper, you'll need a smooth, flat work surface large enough to comfortably rotate your paper and ruler while working. Good overhead lighting is important for viewing your work clearly.

BEST PAPERS FOR PLEATING

Thin paper that holds a crease well works best for pleating because it doesn't need to be scored prior to folding. Scrapbook paper, copy paper, and wrapping paper can all work well. Be sure to test the wrapping paper before using it on your project to be sure that it doesn't have a coating that is prone to cracking when folded. Pleating thick paper is difficult as the paper's bulk makes accurate folding a chore and the pleats often creep out of alignment.

TOOLS FOR PLEATING PAPER

For more information about all of these tools, see pages 17-21.

Steel Ruler and Gridded Cutting Mat
An 18" or 24" steel or steel-edge ruler works well for measuring, and a gridded cutting mat can help speed up the process of marking pleat lines. With a gridded cutting mat, you can align the paper on the grid and use the grid markings to measure the pleat distance(s) along the side edges of the paper.

Pencil, Eraser, and Sharpener
Use a pencil to lightly mark pleat lines on your paper. A mechanical pencil works better than a wooden pencil because the lead is thinner and consistent in size. Use an eraser, such as a Magic Rub brand eraser, for removing pencil markings after pleating. This type of eraser removes markings without marring the paper.

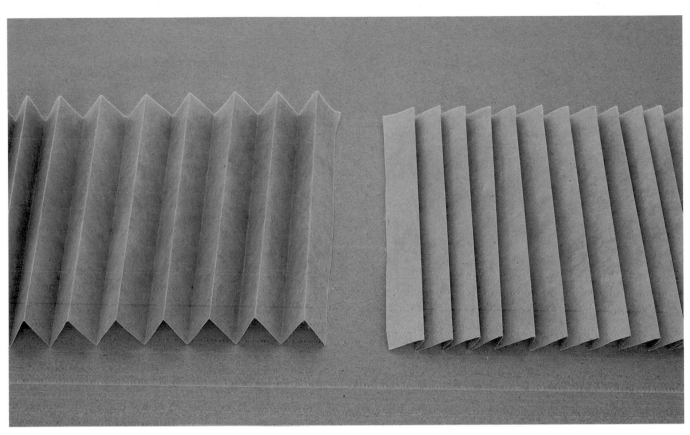

ACCORDION PLEATS (ON LEFT) VERSUS KNIFE PLEATS

Burnisher
A burnisher, such as a bone folder, is used for burnishing the crease lines of the pleats.

Tape
Use masking or drafting tape to temporarily secure paper to your cutting mat to prevent the paper from shifting. Use Scotch removable, clear, low-tack tape for holding pleats in place while working. When finished, the tape easily lifts off without scarring the surface of the paper.

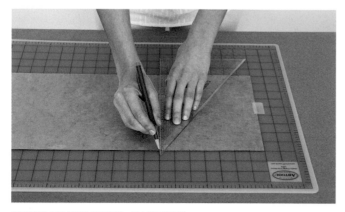

BEFORE FOLDING PLEATS, MARK BOTH
ENDS OF EACH PLEAT ON YOUR PAPER.

AFTER MARKING PLEAT PLACEMENT,
FOLD CAREFULLY.

TIPS FOR PLEATING PAPER

Marking Paper for Pleating

To make pleats across the paper, begin by using a pencil to lightly mark the two ends of each pleat at opposite edges of the paper. If the paper is very large, also mark the center. Horizontal or vertical dash marks are more accurate than tiny dots when marking pleats. If you have a gridded cutting mat, align the paper on the grid, tape it in place with drafting tape, and use the markings on the grid for measuring the pleat distance along the side edges of the paper. Make dash marks at the edges of the paper along the intended fold line. Use a ruler to make dash marks at the center of the paper.

How to Pleat Paper

I prefer to stand when folding a large sheet of paper, so I have a bird's eye view. After marking the paper, lightly fold it using the dash marks as a guide. Gently press the fold line between your fingertips. If the paper is stiff and resists a little, try rolling the paper to make it more malleable. Check for accuracy, then fold sharply along the fold line, using your fingers, or burnish the fold with a burnishing tool. To burnish, draw the narrow, flat edge of the bone folder across the fold line with even pressure to sharply crease the line. If the pleats start getting off, stop and readjust as soon as possible. Small inaccuracies will grow exponentially as you repeat steps.

IF PAPER IS STIFF, GENTLY ROLL AREA TO BE FOLDED TO MAKE IT MORE MALLEABLE AND EASIER TO CREASE ACCURATELY.

CHECK ACCURACY OF FOLD, THEN FOLD SHARPLY, USING FINGERS (AS SHOWN) OR BURNISHING TOOL.

When folding a large project with overlapping pleats, I like to secure the pleats together in a group as I go. For example, after every five pleats I place a long strip of removable Scotch tape perpendicular to the folded edges to keep the pleats in place. This keeps the pleats contained and prevents shifting while I work.

How to Fold Intersecting Pleats

Intersecting pleats, such as on the Pleated Lamp Shade on page 124 and X-Pleat Gift Wrap on page 112, are produced when some pleats are made in one direction, then the paper is rotated and more pleats are made in another direction. The results look complicated, but the steps are exactly the same as for making simple accordion or knife pleats. When you fold the section where the existing pleats cross the new pleat, the paper will be thicker, as there will be several paper layers. Proceed with the pleating process slowly, and pinch each new pleat in place. After pinching the length of each new pleat, sharply crease this length with your fingers or a burnishing tool.

X-Pleat Gift Wrap

Looking to impress the modern minimalist in your life? For the next gift-giving occasion, pick up some beautiful paper, fold the intersecting pleats, and wrap it up (note that solid-colored textured paper shows off the pleat best). If you are including a card or gift tag, tuck it securely into the pleat. No bow required.

SUPPLIES

Practice paper: Any lightweight paper, cut 4" wider and longer than measurement needed to wrap box in traditional way

Gift-wrap paper, cut 4" wider and longer than measurement needed to wrap box in traditional way

Utility scissors

Tape

PAPERS SHOWN
Here and on Page 114

I wrapped the gifts with lokta paper. The envelope is silk-screened chiyogami paper.

Directions

1. Measure the gift-wrap paper needed for the box you're wrapping, and add 4" extra (that is, 2" on all sides) to your width and length measurements before cutting the paper.

2. Lay the paper face down, and rotate it clockwise, so it sits on point.

3. Fold (see Tips for Folding Paper on page 27) the sheet in half, with the crease running diagonally through the left and right corners, and press the crease firmly with your fingers.

4. Create a pleat by mountain-folding (see page 26) the top layer back down about 1" above fold you made in Step 3.

5. Press the pleat firmly, and rotate the paper counter-clockwise so that it sits on the point of the pleat.

6. Fold the sheet in half again, so the crease runs through the left and right corners, and press the crease firmly.

7. Create the second pleat by mountain-folding the top layer back down about 1" above the fold you made in Step 6.

8. Press the pleats firmly, and rotate the paper clockwise so that it sits on one long edge.

9. Center your gift on the intersecting pleats.

10. Wrap the paper around the gift, securing the sides with tape.

11. Wrap each remaining end by folding in the sides of the paper first. Then fold the top edge down and the bottom flap up, and tape the folds shut.

   Add a gift card to one of the pleats, and your package is ready.

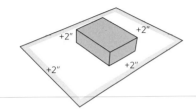

1 INCLUDE EXTRA 4" TO NEEDED
WIDTH AND LENGTH.

2 ROTATE PAPER.

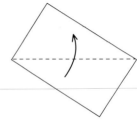

3 FOLD IN HALF DIAGONALLY.

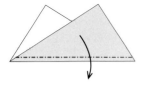

4 FOLD TOP LAYER BACK 1"
ABOVE BOTTOM FOLD.

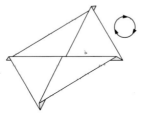

5 PRESS PLEATS, AND
ROTATE PAPER.

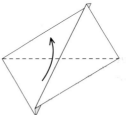

6 FOLD IN HALF DIAGONALLY.

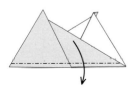

7 FOLD TOP LAYER BACK
1" ABOVE BOTTOM FOLD.

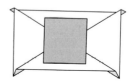

8 PRESS PLEATS, AND
ROTATE PAPER.

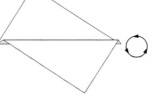

9 CENTER GIFT ON
INTERSECTING PLEATS.

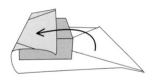

10 WRAP AS USUAL.

11 FOLD SIDES IN, AND
SECURE WITH TAPE.

Chevron
Wall Décor

Zig, zag, zen—this project is the ultimate in pure beauty and really fun to fold. The rhythmic mountain and valley folds are perfect to adorn any wall in your home. It takes a bit of fiddling to get all the zigs and zags to line up in the correct direction, so take your time and enjoy the process. Before tackling this wall décor on a large scale, practice it a few times using printer paper. I recommend a thin, crisp paper for your final masterpiece since it enables you to create super-sharp creases.

FINISHED SIZE

About 34" wide x 26" tall (measurement will vary depending on how far pleating is pulled open)

SUPPLIES

Practice paper: 1 sheet of copy paper

One 30"-wide x 20"-long rectangle of thin, crisp paper (like wrapping paper cut from a roll)

Bone or wood folder

PAPER SHOWN

I made this piece with wrapping paper. I secured it to the wall with a red tack in each corner, then "framed" it with black art tape.

Directions

1. Position the paper horizontally face up, and fold (see Tips for Folding Paper on page 27) the top edge to the bottom edge. Crease the folded edge sharply with a bone folder.

2. Fold only the top layer up in half, and crease the folded edge sharply. Flip the paper over, so the unfolded single layer is on top, and rotate it so that the folds are on the bottom.

3. Fold the top layer down in half.

4. Fold all layers of the top left corner to the bottom edge, crease the folded edge sharply, and unfold it.

5. Fold the bottom edge up to the top point of the crease you made in Step 4. Crease the newly folded edge sharply, and unfold it.

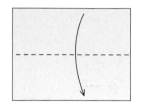

1 FOLD IN HALF.

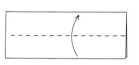

2a FOLD TOP LAYER UP.

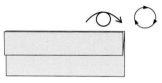

2b FLIP OVER, AND ROTATE.

3a FOLD TOP LAYER DOWN.

3b FOLDED PAPER, WITH FOLDED
EDGES AT TOP.

4a FOLD OVER ALL LEFT
TOP CORNERS.

4b CREASE FOLD SHARPLY,
AND UNFOLD.

5a FOLD BOTTOM EDGE
TO CREASE.

6. Continue to repeat Step 5 to create 45-degree folds across the paper strip.

7. Unfold the sheet of paper entirely to expose a grid of sharp chevron creases across the paper. Refold any creases that look weak—the creases buried inside the paper won't be as sharp as those on the outside since it's hard to crease through the many folded layers at once.

8. This is when the fun begins. You need to reverse every other crease so that you have a series of rows that alternate from mountain to valley folds (see page 26). Follow the drawing at right, making the white lines mountain folds and the black lines valley folds. Start working with the vertical folds on one outside edge first, and work your way down the paper. Even if you find the folding process puzzling at first, be patient and keep working at it—don't give up even if the paper looks messy while you're working. Eventually you'll find that the paper collapses into shape and that the effort was entirely worth the results.

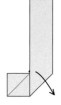

5b CREASE FOLD SHARPLY,
AND UNFOLD.

6 REPEAT STEP 5 ACROSS PAPER.

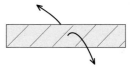

7a UNFOLD PAPER.

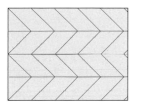

7b SHARPEN WEAK CREASES.

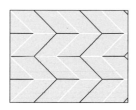

8a REVERSE EVERY OTHER CREASE TO
ALTERNATE MOUNTAIN (WHITE) AND
VALLEY (BLACK) FOLDS.

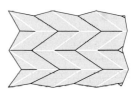

8b IT MAY LOOK MESSY AT FIRST,
BUT PERSIST UNTIL PAPER COLLAPSES
INTO SHAPE.

FOLD PATTERN ON 20" X 30" PAPER

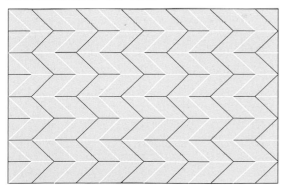

WHITE LINES = MOUNTAIN FOLDS
BLACK LINES = VALLEY FOLDS

Pleated Bowl

This decorative bowl requires very precise pleating, so take your time. To learn the pleating sequence, practice with lightweight paper, which is quicker and easier to fold than medium-weight paper. I call for medium-weight paper for the "real" bowl because it will hold its shape over time.

FINISHED SIZE
11" square

SUPPLIES
Practice paper: 12" square of lightweight paper

One 12" square of medium-weight scrapbook paper, specialty paper, or card stock

1½" square of medium-weight card stock (same paper used for bowl or contrasting paper), for bottom of bowl

Bone or wood folder

Pencil

Ruler

PAPER SHOWN

I made this bowl with printed lokta paper, which makes the bowl fairly delicate. A heavier paper will make a sturdier bowl.

Directions

1. Lay the paper square face up and on point, and fold (see Tips for Folding Paper on page 27) it in half, left to right. Crease the fold sharply with the bone folder, and then unfold it.

2. Fold the paper in half, bottom to top. Crease the fold sharply, unfold it, and flip the paper over.

3. Straighten the square to sit on one edge, and fold the paper in half, left to right. Crease the fold sharply, and unfold it.

4. Fold the paper in half, bottom to top, and crease the fold sharply.

5. Lightly pencil-mark the center of the diagonal creases.

6. Fold the lower right corner up to the center mark on the diagonal crease line, crease the fold sharply, and unfold the paper.

7. Fold the right corner up to the center of the crease line made in Step 6, crease it sharply, and unfold it.

8. Fold the crease line from Step 6 to the original diagonal fold line, sharply crease the new fold, and unfold it. This section of the paper should now be diagonally creased into quarters.

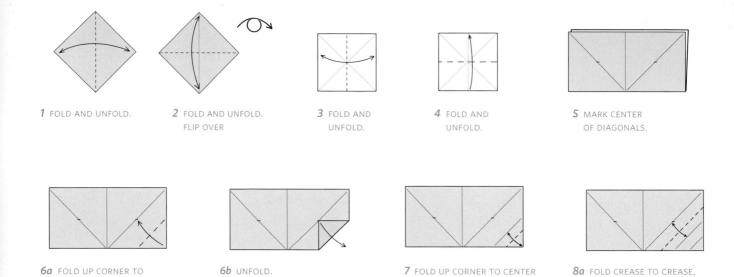

1 FOLD AND UNFOLD.

2 FOLD AND UNFOLD. FLIP OVER

3 FOLD AND UNFOLD.

4 FOLD AND UNFOLD.

5 MARK CENTER OF DIAGONALS.

6a FOLD UP CORNER TO CENTER DIAGONAL.

6b UNFOLD.

7 FOLD UP CORNER TO CENTER OF CREASE, AND UNFOLD.

8a FOLD CREASE TO CREASE, AND UNFOLD.

---

9. Fold each of this section's quarters in half, folding the bottom corner and each crease line to the neighboring crease line, and sharply crease each new fold line.

10. Repeat the folding and unfolding sequence in steps 6-9 on the left bottom corner.

11. Open the paper out flat.

12. Fold the paper in half, from left to right, and lightly pencil-mark the centers of the top and bottom diagonal creases. Rotate the paper counterclockwise, so the fold sits at the bottom.

13. Repeat the folding and unfolding sequence in steps 6-9 on both the bottom right and left corners.

14. Open the paper out flat.

15. Refold the paper on the diagonal.

16. Fold the paper in half again. Rotate the triangle, so it's on point.

17. Fold the bottom point up to the fourth V-crease, fold the new crease sharply, and unfold it.

18. Fold the bottom point up to the second V-crease, fold the new crease sharply, and unfold it.

19. Open the paper out flat.

20. Sharpen the folds (some may have fallen out of shape during bowl's construction) by reworking the crease lines into alternating mountain folds (shown here as white lines) and valley folds (shown as dashed black lines; see page 26 for information on these basic folds). This may look very confusing at first, but focus on the folds. Start at one edge, and you'll soon see the bowl take shape. When you get to the bottom of the bowl, shape the base by pinching the corners of the 1½" square from underneath, which will force the walls of the 3" square to become vertical and cause the sides of the bowl to flare out from the 3" square. As you're working, you may think the bowl looks very messy, but just keep at it, and the bowl will gradually take shape.

21. To keep the bottom of the bowl nice and flat, glue a 1½" square of card stock or paper inside the bottom center of the bowl to reinforce it (and also hide any problem folds at the bottom).

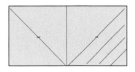

8b SECTION IS EVENLY
QUARTERED.

9 FOLD EACH QUARTER IN
HALF, AND UNFOLD.

10 REPEAT STEPS 5-9 ON
LEFT SIDE.

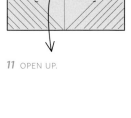

11 OPEN UP.

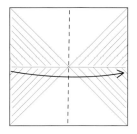

12a FOLD PAPER IN HALF.

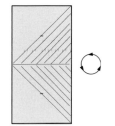

12b MARK CENTERS OF TOP
AND BOTTOM CREASES,
AND ROTATE.

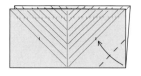

13 REPEAT STEPS 5-9
ON BOTTOM CORNERS.

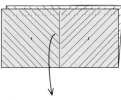

14 OPEN UP.

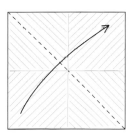

15 FOLD IN HALF DIAGONALLY.

16 FOLD IN HALF.
ROTATE.

17 FOLD TIP TO
4TH CREASE,
AND UNFOLD.

18 FOLD TIP TO
2ND CREASE,
AND UNFOLD.

19 OPEN UP.

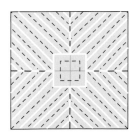

20a SHARPEN FOLDS AND REVERSE EVERY
OTHER CREASE TO ALTERNATE
MOUNTAIN (WHITE) AND VALLEY
(DASHED BLACK) FOLDS.

20b KEEP WORKING AT SHARPENING
ALTERNATE FOLDS UNTIL BOWL
TAKES SHAPE.

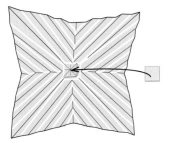

21 GLUE IN PAPER SQUARE TO
REINFORCE CENTER BOTTOM.

Pleated Lamp Shade

Because paper is somewhat rigid and requires only minimal interior framing, it is perfect for making lamp shades. You start this project with a rectangular sheet of paper, pleat it in two different directions, and then, to make a sphere, reshape the pleats by arching them open one row at a time—no cutting · involved. It's a really cool process with beautiful results.

FINISHED SIZE

About 4" wide at top x 5½" tall at center point

SUPPLIES

Practice paper: One 8½"-wide x 11"-long sheet of copy paper

One 24"-wide x 37"-long rectangle of thin, crisp, translucent paper

24" metal ruler

Pencil

Bone or wood folder

Removable tape

Glue stick

⅛"-round paper punch

Kitchen twine

PAPER SHOWN

I made these lamp shades with kozo paper with strands of hemp.

Directions

1. Measure and mark the outside edges of the practice paper. Then, starting at the top of the paper and working your way down, fold (see Tips for Folding Paper on page 27) the marked alternating mountain and valley folds (see page 26) in Drawing 1. Use a bone folder to crease the folded edges flat. The resulting pleats will overlap, like pleats in a kilt.

2. In this step the pleating technique produces stacked pleats all the same size that sit atop one another like pleats in a closed fan. Mark 1" increments for 7" at the top and bottom edges. Starting on the left edge and working across the paper, mountain-fold and then valley-fold the marked lines. Use a bone folder to firmly crease the folded edges flat. Then rotate the paper, so it's horizontal, with the long extending edge positioned at the back.

3. Holding the paper firmly where marked with stars, pull the center pleats, and then the surrounding pleats, outward in an arc. Continue to shape the paper by arching the pleats of each row. Isn't that cool? I love shaping these pleats and seeing a sphere emerge (note that the practice sheet produces a quarter-slice of a sphere).

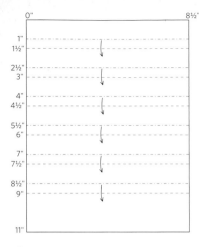

1a MEASURE AND MARK PRACTICE PAPER.

1b ALTERNATE FOLDING MOUNTAIN AND VALLEY FOLDS TO MAKE KNIFE PLEATS.

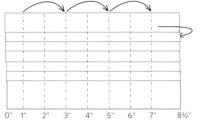

2a ACCORDION-PLEAT ACROSS PAPER, MAKING FIRST MOUNTAIN, THEN VALLEY FOLDS.

2b ROTATE PAPER.

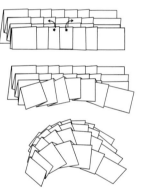

3 HOLD FIRMLY AT CENTER, AND PULL PLEATS OUTWARD IN ARC.

4 REPEAT STEP 1 WITH PROJECT PAPER, AND USE REMOVABLE TAPE TO KEEP PLEATS IN PLACE.

5-8 REPEAT STEP 2, PUNCH HOLE AT TOP LEFT, AND THREAD WITH TWINE. REMOVE TAPE, GLUE EDGE, AND SHAPE SPHERE.

4. Now that you have successfully completed the practice pleats, repeat Step 1 to measure and mark your paper for the lamp shade. To reinforce the paper's top edge, fold this edge 1" to the back side so that the shade's edge will be double-layered. Continue to work your way down the paper as you did with the practice paper, mountain-folding and valley-folding the marked lines. Since this paper is much larger than your practice sheet, I suggest using removable tape to hold the pleats in place as you work. Otherwise the pleats can splay out, and things can get out of whack quickly. To secure the pleats, place long vertical strips of tape across several pleats at a time, spacing the tape about every 8" to 10".

5. Repeat step 2 to fold the vertical stacked pleats every inch, alternating the mountain and valley folds and stacking the pleats accurately atop one another. In the left upper corner of the stacked pleats, punch a hole about ¼" down and in from the edge through all the pleats.

ATTACHING SHADE TO LIGHTING FIXTURE

When attaching this lamp shade to a light source, always follow the UL-recommended maximum wattage on the fixture and shade. Do not use this shade with a halogen or quartz lamp as they get much too hot.

The least complicated way to use this shade is to slip it over a premade shade, adhering the two by placing beads of tack glue, such as Aleene's Tacky Glue, at the top and bottom edges of the premade shade. Don't cinch the top or bottom of your shade tightly. Leave an opening, so the heat from the bulb can escape and air can circulate.

The other option is to secure the pleated shade to a metal frame. For the pendant-style lamp pictured, purchase a frame fitted with a butterfly clip that snaps over the bulb. Using a needle threaded with cord, stitch around the inside edge, catching both the lamp shade and the ring at the top of the frame with each stitch. Again, don't cinch the top or bottom tightly, and leave an opening, so the heat from the bulb can escape and air can circulate.

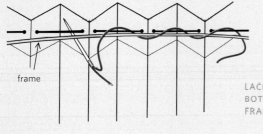

frame

LACE THE CORD AROUND BOTH THE SHADE AND FRAME.

6. Thread a piece of twine through the hole, and cinch the top of the shade. Loosely tie the twine in a bow rather than a knot since you may need to adjust the size of the opening.

7. To begin shaping the sphere, remove the tape securing the pleats, and overlap the end pleats, right over left, so the seam sits in the valley of the pleat. Once you've seen how to position the seam, lift up the upper edge, and swipe glue stick along the lower edge. Reposition the edges to make the seam, this time interlocking the horizontal pleats on the back of one edge with the horizontal pleats on the front of the other edge, so the form appears continuous. Pinch the top and bottom edges together until the glue sets.

8. Once the glue has set, repeat step 3 to shape the sphere. Holding the paper firmly, pull each pleat in one row outward in an arc. Continue shaping the pleats of each row into arcs. Take your time as you move through the shaping process, and be sure that the shade is evenly shaped on all sides (looking at the shape in profile will help you see if it's balanced).

I like to hang this shade as one of a group of pendant lights, placing it over an inexpensive shade that's fire-resistant. And keep in mind that the heat from the bulb needs to escape through the top of the shade, so don't cinch the top too tight.

Chapter 6

RECYCLING

ROW 1: ORIGAMI PAPER, GROCERY LIST, CORRUGATED CARDBOARD

ROW 2: GIFT WRAP, MAP, BIRTHDAY CARD

ROW 3: CATALOG, TAKE-OUT MENU, NEWSPAPER

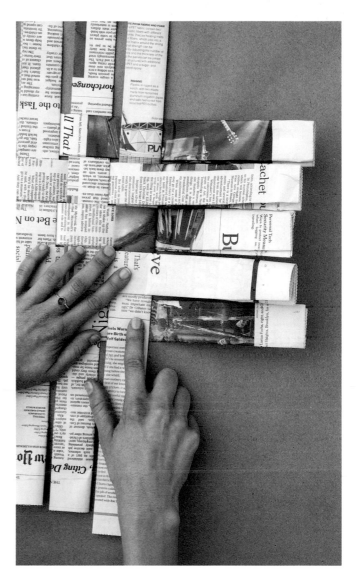

Recycled paper has been inspiring creative people for ages. Think of papier-mâché, decoupage, even the gum-wrapper weaving taught at summer camps. I was fascinated to see paper jewelry made from triangles of magazine paper made by women in Uganda and amazed to learn that they were following a paper beading tradition practiced by women in Victorian England (who made beaded room dividers out of wallpaper). Architect Frank Gehry made furniture out of corrugated cardboard. My *Origami Page-A-Day Calendar* started as a way to recycle the pages from another page-a-day calendar. Take a moment to rethink, repurpose, and reuse paper. Why not give it a whirl—it's free.

BEST PAPERS FOR RECYCLED PAPER PROJECTS

The best place to start looking for recycled papers is your own mailbox. Newspapers, catalogs, magazines, corrugated boxes, and paper packing materials are all potential sources of free materials that you can use in your paper crafting projects. Choose thinner papers for folding and pleating, and select thicker papers for scoring projects. For best results, try to match the type of paper to what is recommended in a project's Supplies list. Maps and unwanted posters are a colorful source of large paper and can be used for X-Pleat Gift Wrap (page 112). Old Christmas cards are perfect for making the Garland Chain on page 66. Foreign newspapers, comics, and grocery circulars can add a pop of style and are fun to incorporate into projects such as the Newspaper Basket (page 130) and the Wine-Bottle Daisy Frill (page 54). Calendar pages and magazine covers often have a durable coating, which might prove to be a good characteristic for some projects. Try using them to make the Candy Cones on page 28. Also consider packaging, such as cereal and cracker boxes, which could be used to make the Treat Boxes on page 36. Just about any paper has the potential to be recycled.

There are so many different papers to consider for reuse. In this chapter I picked a couple of my favorites and created some projects that, hopefully, will inspire you to try a recycled project of your own.

Newspaper Basket

My mentor and friend, Florence Temko, taught me how to make this woven newspaper basket. I enlarged the shape, but the simple genius of using recycled newspaper for this project is all Temko.

Note: You may want to grab a few extra sheets of newspaper because you will surely run across an interesting article that you will want to save and read later.

FINISHED SIZE
10" wide x 11½" long x 5" deep

SUPPLIES
Practice paper: Newspaper

21 full (23"-wide x 22"-long) sheets of newspaper (I like the *New York Times*)

Metal straightedge (optional)

Bone or wood folder

Binder clips

Glue stick

Utility scissors

Directions

1. Start with a full-size sheet of newspaper (like the *New York Times*, not a smaller tabloid paper) folded in half along the existing vertical crease. Continue to narrow the sheet by folding it in half vertically three more times to yield a strip with 16 layers. To make a strip that will produce a neat basket, fold the strip's raw edges to the inside as follows: Unfold the last two folds, refold both outside edges to the center crease, and then fold it once more. Then use a bone folder to sharply crease the edges flat. Repeat the folding process with 20 more pages of newspaper to get 21 strips total. (You may want to wash your hands—and the bone folder—after folding all the strips since you'll have the newsprint ink on them and anything else you touch afterwards.)

2. Start your basket by creating its bottom as follows: Lay seven folded strips side by side vertically, aligning the top and bottom edges and placing the most interesting sides of the strips face down, so they show on the outside of your basket. Note that because the strips tend to shift, you may want to place a heavy object like a metal straight-edge ruler on top of them to hold them in position as you work.

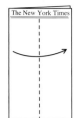

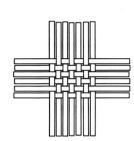

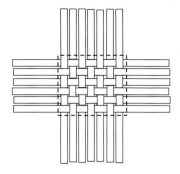

1a FOLD IN HALF VERTICALLY
THREE TIMES.

1b FOLD 21 STRIPS TOTAL.

2 POSITION 7 STRIPS, AND WEAVE 6
STRIPS OVER AND UNDER THEM.

3 PREPARE SIDES BY FOLDING UP
UNWOVEN ENDS.

Starting about 5″ from the top edge, weave one strip horizontally over and under the vertical strips. Then similarly weave in five more horizontal strips , alternating whether you start over or under the outermost vertical strip. As you work, snug each new strip up next to the one just woven, and try using binder clips to keep neighboring strips in place. Straighten out the strips as you work and then again after you're finished.

3. Fold up the unwoven ends of the strips in preparation for weaving the sides of the basket (even if they don't stay put vertically, this initial fold readies them for Step 5).

4. To create double-length strips for weaving the basket's sides, start by joining two of the remaining eight strips, overlapping each pair's ends

by 1″, securing the join with a swipe or two of the glue stick, and using a binder clip to hold the join in place until the glue dries. Repeat the process so that you have four double-length strips.

5. Interweave the basket's sides with separate double-length strips, using the same under-over weaving technique as before and finishing each strip by swiping the glue stick on its end, overlapping the end over the beginning of the same strip, and using a binder clip to hold the join in place until the glue dries.

Then start the next strip above the one you just wove, positioning it to start so that it correctly keeps the over-under weave pattern going. End the strip just as you did with the first round.

Add one more double-length strip to finish weaving the basket's sides. Then even out the sides by pulling and tightening up the gaps between the strips.

6. Trim off the ends of any strips that extend above the top edge of the basket.

7. Unfold the last double-length strip once to open it out, and generously swipe glue stick on its inner edges. Then slip the opened strip over the basket's top edge to encase and bind its raw edges and give the basket a finished look. Overlap the ends of the binding strip, and trim them, if needed, for a clean finish. Then use a few binder clips around the basket's edge to hold the binding tightly in place until the glue dries completely.

1"

4 GLUE 2 STRIPS TOGETHER FOR
WEAVING SIDES; MAKE 4 TOTAL.

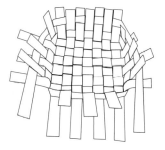

5a WEAVE SIDES WITH SAME
OVER-UNDER PATTERN.

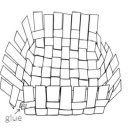

glue

5b GLUE ENDS TOGETHER;
ADD NEXT STRIP.

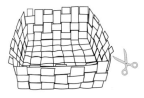

6 ADJUST STRIPS EVENLY;
CUT OFF EXTRA BITS.

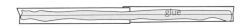

glue

7a APPLY GLUE TO INSIDE OF
LAST STRIP.

7b BIND TOP EDGE WITH
LAST STRIP.

Corrugated Room Screen

Strategically cut and folded corrugated cardboard sections are slotted into each other to create this more than five-foot-tall room screen. Use it to add visual interest to a room, as a partition, or to hide unpacked boxes after a big move. Uncomplicated, sturdy, and elegant, this is one of my all-time favorite projects.

FINISHED SIZE

5' 4" square (or can be pulled out a little to lengthen it)

SUPPLIES

Practice paper: 1 large corrugated box

Four 20"-wide x 20"-long x 24"-deep corrugated boxes

24" metal ruler

X-Acto knife

Large cutting mat (24" wide x 36" long is best)

Pencil

Directions

1. Working with one box at a time, break down the ends of the box, so it lies flat. Using a metal ruler, X-Acto knife, and cutting mat, carefully cut the flaps off the box, cleanly cutting through both layers. Save the flaps for practice cutting in step 4.

2. Place your cutting mat inside the box, and slice along the box's seamed edge, cutting carefully just through the box's top layer. Open the box up flat and face up.

3. On each 20" panel, measure and pencil-mark a center line at the 10" point. Take note of the cardboard's vertical corrugated pattern, which will serve as a good guide for keeping your marked lines and folds straight. To bend the marked center line of each panel, position the center line on the edge of a table; place a metal ruler on top of the line; hold the cardboard and ruler securely in place; and, with even pressure, bend the cardboard hanging off the table up towards you at a right angle. Don't fold the cardboard all the way over on itself since that will cause unwanted creasing; just bend the cardboard up into an L shape. After creasing the first panel, repeat the process to crease the rest of the panels.

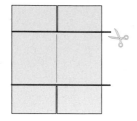

1 CUT FLAPS OFF BOX.

2 CUT OPEN SEAMED EDGE.

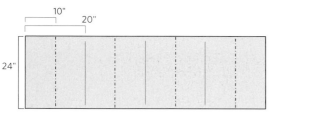

3 MEASURE AND MARK CENTER OF EACH
PANEL, AND FOLD PANEL UP AT RIGHT ANGLE.

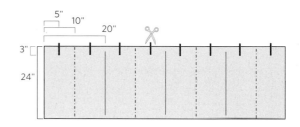

4 MEASURE AND MARK CENTER
OF EACH 10" PANEL, AND CUT 3" SLOTS.

4. Measure and mark the top edge of each 10" panel at its 5" center point. Starting at that center point, measure and mark 3" down from the top edge, positioning your line along one of the vertical corrugated channels, which will serve as a guide to help keep things straight. Straddling the center line, cut a slot 3" long and about ⅛" wide. The width of your cut depends on the thickness of your cardboard—the thicker the cardboard, the wider the cut line needs to be. When assembling the screen, you'll fit one panel into slots on a neighboring panel, and the fit of the slot should be snug but not so tight that it pinches or presses and warps the cardboard panel. To determine the right width for the slot, test it out using two of the flaps you cut off in Step 1. Make a ⅛"-wide by 3"-long slot in one flap, and insert the second flap into the slot. If the fit seems too tight—or too loose—adjust the width of the slots you make in your actual screen panel accordingly.

5. In the drawing at right, you'll see that the screen is made up of five panels (labeled A-E), each a different height. The first panel you worked with in steps 1-4 is left full-height and labeled Panel A. To create the other panels, start by repeating Step 1 above on the

remaining three boxes. Then set aside one of the three trimmed boxes for a second full-height (24") panel, which becomes Panel C.

Then, before repeating Step 2 to cut open the seam on the two remaining boxes, cut these boxes into panels the following heights, cutting cleanly through the two layers of each box at once: Panel B, 16"; Panel D, 12"; and Panel E, 8" (note that you'll have 2 scraps left over, 4" and 6").

Then repeat steps 2-4 on each of the remaining panels. Note that, when cutting the slots into the panels, you'll cut slots into the top and bottom edges of the middle panels (B, C, and D) only. Panel A gets slotted on the top edge only, and Panel E gets cut on the bottom edge only.

6. To assemble the screen, first position the panels in alphabetical order, with Panel A on the bottom. Next fold Panel B so that it zigzags in the opposite order from Panel A. Then fold panels C and E, so they zigzag like Panel A, and fold Panel D to zigzag like Panel B. Slide Panel B into the slots at the top of Panel A (note that slightly compressing the zigzagging takes the pressure off the slots and makes it easier to slip the panels together). Then slide Panel C into the slots at the top of Panel B, and continue working in this fashion until you've assembled all the panels.

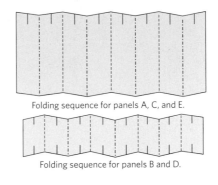

Folding sequence for panels A, C, and E.

Folding sequence for panels B and D.

5-6 FOLDING SEQUENCES FOR PANEL

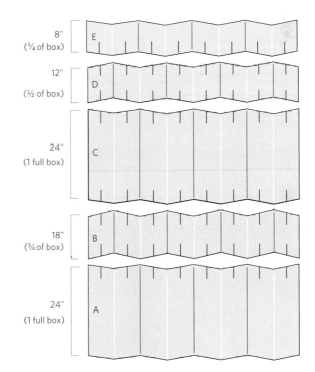

8"
(⅓ of box) — E

12"
(½ of box) — D

24"
(1 full box) — C

18"
(¾ of box) — B

24"
(1 full box) — A

SCREEN ASSEMBLY

Hexagon Storage Bin

I love working with corrugated cardboard. The color, the size, the rigidity, even the smell—they're all good to me. While creating the other corrugated projects for this book, I collected a huge stack of box flaps. Unable to just toss them, I came up with this six-sided storage bin using six flaps. If the surface color of the cardboard doesn't go with your décor, try painting it with water-soluble craft paint and a small roller.

FINISHED SIZE
9½" diameter x 14" tall

SUPPLIES
Practice paper: Two box flaps cut off box in Step 1

One 14"-square corrugated box

Large cutting mat (24" wide x 36" long is best)

24" metal ruler

X-Acto knife

Pencil

Eraser

Photocopied template (see Step 5) or 1 sheet of newspaper

Masking tape

Glue stick or white tacky glue

Directions

1. Lay the box flat on the cutting mat. Using the metal ruler and X-Acto knife, carefully cut the flaps off the box, cleanly cutting through both layers. You'll end up with eight 7"-wide x 14"-long flaps and the center section of the box. You'll need six of the flaps, leaving two for practice. Save the center section for Step 4.

2. To cut a tab in the first flap, position the flap face up, and measure and lightly pencil-mark 1" in on both the top and bottom edges on both short sides. Then, on the right side, mark 2" down from the top edge and 4" up from the bottom edge. Next draw a line from the 1" mark down to the 2" mark, and another line from the 2" mark out to meet the 1" line. Repeat the process on the bottom right corner with the 1" and 4" marks you just made. Then use the metal ruler and X-Acto knife to carefully cut away these corner sections, leaving a tab on this side.

   To cut the slit on the left side of the flap, mark 1½" down from the top edge and 3½" up from the bottom edge. Carefully cut a 9"-long slit about ⅛" wide, positioning it 1" in from the left side and starting 1½" from the top edge.

1a CUT FLAPS OFF BOX.

1b SAVE CENTER SECTION FOR LATER.

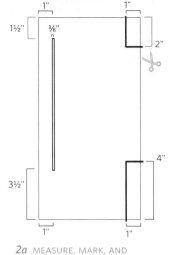

1" 1"

1½" ⅛"

2"

3½"

4"

1" 1"

2a MEASURE, MARK, AND CUT FLAP.

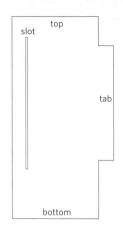

slot top

tab

bottom

2b USE FLAP AS TEMPLATE TO CUT 5 MORE FLAPS.

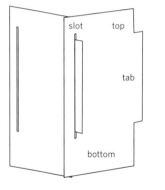

slot top

tab

bottom

3 CONNECT FLAPS BY INSERTING TAB IN SLOT.

4 CUT BOX OPEN ON SEAMED EDGE, AND CUT OFF 1 PANEL.

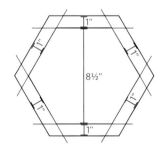

1"

1" 1"

8½"

1" 1"

1"

5 MEASURE AND MARK 1" IN FROM ALL SIDES. DRAW LINE ALONG EACH SIDE AT THIS POINT.

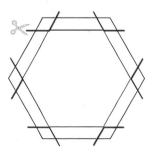

6a CUT OUT CORNERS OF HEXAGON.

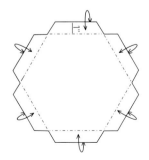

6b FOLD AND UNFOLD FLAPS.

glue

7 APPLY GLUE, SLIDE IN POSITION FROM BOTTOM OF HEXAGON.

MAKING A TEMPLATE FOR
THE HEXAGONAL BOTTOM

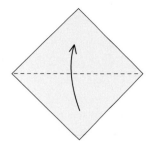

1 FOLD 12" SQUARE
IN HALF.

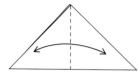

2 FOLD TRIANGLE IN HALF,
AND THEN UNFOLD.

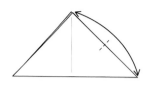

3 PINCH FOLD IN CENTER
OF EDGE.

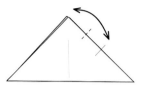

4 PINCH FOLD IN CENTER
OF EDGE'S UPPER HALF.

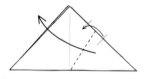

5 FOLD RIGHT SIDE ACROSS TO
LEFT, ALIGNING CREASES MADE
IN STEPS 3 AND 4 AS A GUIDE.

6 FOLD LEFT SIDE
OVER RIGHT.

5¼"

7a CUT STRAIGHT LINE
ACROSS ALL LAYERS, AND
OPEN UP PAPER.

7b COMPLETED TEMPLATE.

You can now use this first completed flap as a template for tracing the cut lines on the remaining flaps. After you finish, erase any remaining pencil marks on the flaps.

3. Insert the tab of one flap into the slit of another flap, and repeat the process until you've joined all six flaps in a circle.

4. Cut open the center of the box, and cut off one panel to use to make the storage bin's hexagonal bottom.

5. To make the hexagonal bottom, enlarge the hexagon template in Drawing 5 by 850% (or enlarge it two times—first by 400% and then by 210%). Alternatively, follow the directions above to make your own pattern from newspaper. Use masking tape to tape your completed pattern to the panel you cut off in Step 4, and cut out the hexagonal bottom.

Then measure 1" in from all six sides, and draw a straight line along each side at this point.

6. Carefully cut out each of the six corners made by the intersecting lines drawn in Step 5. Fold each of the flaps to the back, and then unfold them.

7. Swipe each flap with glue stick or white tacky glue. With the flaps pointed down (so the glue will adhere to the sides of the storage bin), slide the storage bin's new base up into the hexagonal cylinder from the bottom by about 1". The fit should be snug.

Resources

The materials and and tools used in the projects in this book are generally available at art supply, craft, and paper stores nationwide. Below I've listed some of my favorite stores in cities I frequent as well as online sources.

Art Essentials
32 E. Victoria St.
Santa Barbara, CA 93101
805-965-5456
www.sbartessentials.com
The staff here is very knowledgeable.

Flax
1699 Market St.
San Francisco, CA 94103
415-552-2355
www.flaxart.com
The legendary paper room is well worth a road trip.

Hiromi Paper, Inc.
Bergamot Station
2525 Michigan Ave., G-9
Santa Monica, CA 90404
310-998-0098
www.hiromipaper.com
An amazing source of handmade papers from all over the world.

Kate's Paperie
72 Spring St.
New York, NY 10012
212-941-9816
www.katespaperie.com
Beautiful selection of decorative papers.

A.C. Moore
www.acmoore.com
Retail stores nationwide.

Dick Blick Art Materials
www.dickblick.com

Jo-Ann Fabric and Craft
www.joann.com
Retail stores nationwide.

The Lamp Shop
www.lampshop.com
Lamp-making supplies for Pleated Lamp Shade on page 124.

Michael's Stores
www.michaels.com

Paper Arts
www.paperarts.com
Fun collection of decorative papers that can be sorted by color.

Paper Source
www.paper-source.com
Inspiring selection of paper, supplies, and tools. Retail stores nationwide.

Pearl Paint
www.pearlpaint.com

Books About Paper and Paper Crafting

Papermaking: The History and Technique of an Ancient Craft by Dard Hunter (Dover) First published in 1934, an oldie but a real goodie.

Paper: Tear, Fold, Rip, Crease, Cut by Raven Smith (Black Dog) Paper in contemporary art, fashion, and design.

Which Paper? A Guide to Choosing Fine Papers for Artists, Craftspeople, and Designers by Silvie Turner (estamp)

The Joy of Origami by Margaret Van Sicklen (Workman) An origami primer.

Origami Boxes by Florence Temko (Tuttle) Temko's instructions are always easy to follow.

Origami Tessellations: Awe-Inspiring Geometric Designs by Eric Gjerde (AK Peters) Incredible folded mosaics that must be seen.

Thought-Provoking Books and Magazines

Tony Duquette by Wendy Goodman and Hutton Wilkinson (Abrams) An imagination like no other.

Tord Boontje by Martina Margetts (Rizzoli) Beautiful photos of Boontje's work.

World of Interiors A British monthly magazine; any issue past or present will do. www.worldofinteriors.co.uk

ACKNOWLEDGMENTS

Thanks to STC Craft/Melanie Falick Books for giving me the opportunity to present paper crafts in a modern light. I am so thrilled to be under the guidance of Melanie Falick, whose gorgeous craft books have blown the dust off the category. Thanks to Jen Gotch for her double contribution as stylist and photographer. Her sense of color is glamorous and her photographs dreamy. Thanks to onethread, the graphic design studio that pulled together all of the pieces so beautifully. And 22 big thanks to my crackerjack tech editor, Chris Timmons, whose passion for clarity is just amazing.

Special thanks to the Santa Barbara firefighters, who saved the house and these projects from going up in smoke during the Jesusita Fire; to Mary J. Blige, whose music has kept this project pumping; and to my favorite insect, the paper wasp, for just being its ingenious self.

Thanks, Sven, for all your love and support. You're my A Plan guy.

Margaret Van Sicklen is a designer, paper artist, and author. She created the bestselling annual *Origami Page-A-Day Calendar* and is the author of two previous paper-craft books: *The Joy of Origami* and *Origami on the Go*. She is currently concocting new projects in her paper-filled studio in Santa Barbara, California. Visit her website at www.modernpapercrafts.com.